New England Now

CONTEMPORARY

ART

FROM

SIX STATES

1987

DeCordova and Dana Museum and Park
Lincoln, Massachusetts

The Currier Gallery of Art
Manchester, New Hampshire

David Winton Bell Gallery
Brown University, Providence, Rhode Island

Bowdoin College Museum of Art
Brunswick, Maine

The New Britain Museum of American Art
New Britain, Connecticut

Robert Hull Fleming Museum
University of Vermont, Burlington, Vermont

New England Now

New England Now presents some of the most significant and challenging contemporary work by New England artists. Strange to say, nothing of its kind has been attempted here before. Perhaps there was felt no need. The region has long languished in the shadow of New York. Good art was Manhattan-made. Reflecting this attitude, New England art museums often failed to treat seriously the art made in their own province. But provincialism does not have the derisive connotations of even a decade ago. The devolution of the art world has spurred the rise of many vital regional centers. It is no longer true—if it ever was true—that the best artists live in New York. Nowadays, the best live everywhere and a good many live in New England. This exhibition features twenty-five.

Once codenamed the "Minus Manhattan Project," this exhibition is the collaborative effort of six museums, one from each of the New England states. Selection of the artists was made by a committee of curators representing the participating institutions. First, each curator presented the work of artists from his or her state. Then, collectively, we narrowed the field to a manageable number. Judgments were based solely on the merits of the work, without reference to medium, style, theme, or the celebrity of the artist. Large-scale sculpture and environments were considered, and three projects were commissioned for installation at individual museums.

Surveying the selections, we found no unifying theme, no attitude, no *look* that could be called *New English*. The dizzying eclecticism of this exhibition mirrors the diversity of the contemporary visual arts in the region. It is the intention of this show to celebrate that diversity.

A project of this ambition is the labor of many. First and foremost, we are grateful to the artists, their galleries, and their patrons for their willingness to lend to an extended tour. In organizing the myriad details of a traveling exhibition, we were capably assisted by the staffs of our museums. Though their numbers do not permit a full listing, we especially wish to thank Helen S. Dubé, clerk/typist, and Elizabeth A. Mullen '88, student assistant, at the Bowdoin College Museum of Art; Judith E. Tolnick, curator, at the David Winton Bell Gallery; Marilyn F. Hoffman, director of The Currier Gallery of Art; Barbara Stecher, program specialist, and Gillian Titus, curatorial intern, at the DeCordova and Dana Museum and Park; and David Penney, registrar, and Ann Porter, acting curator, at the Robert Hull Fleming Museum. The publication of the catalogue was supervised by Lucie G. Teegarden and Rachel D. Dutch of the Bowdoin College Office of Public Relations and Publications. Susan L. Ransom edited the text. The design is by Michael W. Mahan.

Financial support for this exhibition has been provided by each of the six museums. Additional funding has been received from Analog Devices and Lechmere, Inc.

Lastly, we wish to acknowledge the fundamental contribution of Amy Lighthill, who three years ago helped get this show aloft before parachuting to safety.

John W. Coffey
Bowdoin College
Museum of Art

Robert M. Doty
The Currier Gallery of Art

Daniel C. DuBois
The New Britain Museum
of American Art

Ildiko Heffernan
Robert Hull Fleming Museum,
University of Vermont

Rachel Rosenfield Lafo
DeCordova and Dana
Museum and Park

Nancy R. Versaci
David Winton Bell Gallery
Brown University

Pat Adams

Pat Adams claims she cannot remember a time when she was not painting. Even though she is a teacher, mother, and wife, she finds that it is painting that gives form to her life. In 1977 she wrote, "I have chosen the visual stuffs of color, surface, place, extent, direction, and amount to find out something about the impersonal self, about the parameter of being."

Raised in California, Adams spent several years in New York City and some time in Europe. She moved to Vermont in 1964 to teach painting at Bennington College, where she lives in a turn-of-the-century cottage surrounded by Vermont's Green Mountains. It is a place where idyllic nature is shaped and nurtured by the hand of man; a place where the seasons and weather constantly change the basic elements of the landscape. It is a place one feels in her paintings.

Pat Adams was influenced early on by Alfred Barnes's *The Art of Painting.* She has always worked in an abstract mode, and her work has been "beautiful" in an era when beauty in art has been suspect. She layers, blots, and dissolves the oil and acrylic paints with turpentine, extends her colors and surfaces with mica to catch the light, and creates visual ambiguities. The geometric regularity of her circles and arches is achieved by using a monoprint technique. She uses her hands, sponges, and cloths as well as the brush, while staining, scraping, and encrusting materials to create a range of textures.

Adams is represented in this exhibition by one of her large paintings and a series of small works on paper. *Rerum* is one of her recent paintings, with planetlike "worlds" overlapping and circling one another. Grainy particles of mica and shell are suspended with isobutyl methacrylate as a clear binder. The small paintings, completed in 1987 but begun at different times, function as poetic metaphors.

I.H.

Born 1928 in Stockton, California
Education: University of California,
Berkeley, California; B.A., 1949
Residence: Bennington, Vermont
Current position: Member of the art
faculty, Bennington College

Selected Individual Exhibitions
1987 Maryland Institute, College of Art, Meyerhoff Gallery, College Park, Maryland, *Artist/Printmaker*

1986 Haggin Museum, Stockton, California, *Pat Adams: Selected Works on Paper 1976-1985*

Zabriskie Gallery, New York, New York, and Paris, France. Biannual exhibitions since 1960.

1982 Columbia Museum, Columbia, South Carolina, *Works on Paper*

1979 Contemporary Arts Center, Cincinnati, Ohio, *Pat Adams: Paintings: Survey 1952-1979*

1978 Robert Hull Fleming Museum, University of Vermont, Burlington, Vermont, *Pat Adams: Works on Paper*

1966 Middlebury College, Middlebury, Vermont, *Pat Adams Selected Works*

Selected Group Exhibitions
1984 Robert Hull Fleming Museum, University of Vermont, Burlington, Vermont, *Contemporary Artists in Vermont*

1983 The Chrysler Museum, Norfolk, Virginia, *Aspects of Color*

1982 Museum of Fine Arts, Boston, Massachusetts, *Graham Gund Collection: A Private Vision*

Museum of Fine Arts, Houston, Texas, *Miró in America*

1979 The Art Institute of Chicago, Chicago, Illinois, *100 Artists—100 Years*

1974 Hirshhorn Museum and Sculpture Garden, Washington, D.C., *Inaugural Exhibition*

1961, 1956 Whitney Museum of American Art, New York, New York, *Annual Exhibition*

Selected Bibliography
1986 Emmie Donadio. "Night Flight to Byzantium: The New Works of Pat Adams." *Arts Magazine* 60 (June 1986), pp. 38-39.

1984 Eleanor Tufts. *American Women Artists, Past and Present: A Selected Bibliographic Guide.* Garland Publishing, 1984, pp. 4-5.

1982 John Russell. "Miró's Impact in America." *New York Times,* June 13, 1982, pp. H45, H48.

1979 John Yau. "Pat Adams at Zabriskie." *Art in America* 67 (May/June 1979), p. 142.

1978 Richard Lorber. "Pat Adams' Modernity." *Artforum* 16 (Summer 1978), pp. 38-41.

Selected Fellowships and Awards
1986 Award in Art, American Academy and Institute of Arts and Letters

1984 Distinguished Teaching of Art Award, College Art Association

1976, 1968 Fellowship, National Endowment for the Arts

1972, 1968 Residency Fellowship, The MacDowell Colony, Peterborough, New Hampshire

1970, 1969, 1964, 1954 Residency Fellowship, Yaddo Foundation, Saratoga Springs, New York

1959 Fulbright Fellowship

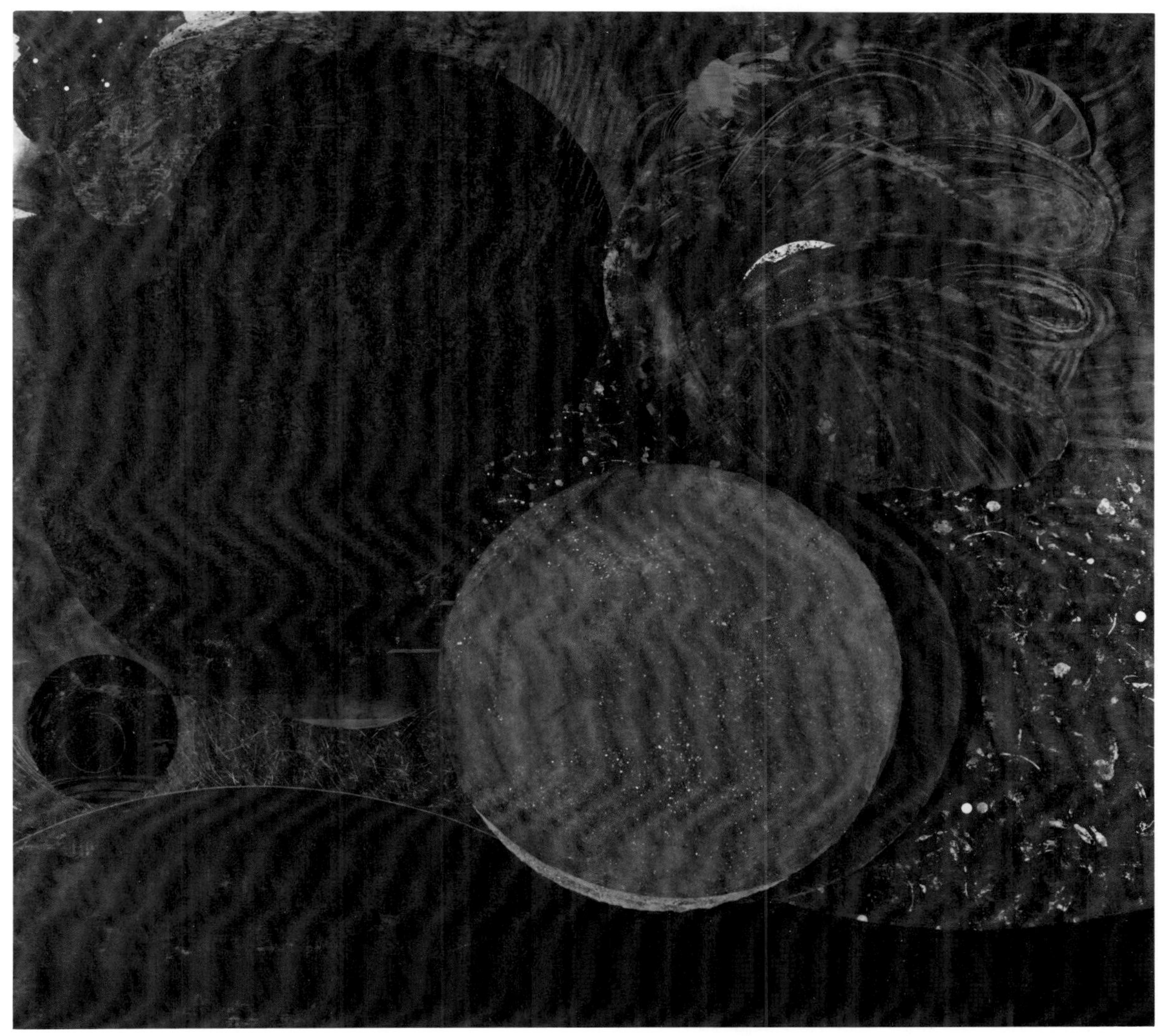

Bring to Mind, 1987
acrylic on paper with shell and sand
8 x 9⅞ inches
Lent by Zabriskie Gallery

Dark Pass, 1987
acrylic on paper with shell and sand
7⅞ x 10⅜ inches
Lent by Zabriskie Gallery

* *Rerum,* 1987
oil on double primed linen, isobutyl, oil
methacrylate, shell, and sand
71½ x 78 inches
Lent by Zabriskie Gallery,
New York, New York

IS:SI, 1987
acrylic on paper with shell and sand
7 x 14 inches
Lent by Zabriskie Gallery

Pleasure's Roll, 1987
acrylic on paper with shell and sand
8 x 8 inches
Lent by Zabriskie Gallery

Other, 1987
acrylic on paper with shell and sand
8¾ x 13⅜ inches
Lent by Zabriskie Gallery

Time Gathering, 1987
acrylic on paper with shell and sand
6 x 13⅜ inches
Lent by Zabriskie Gallery

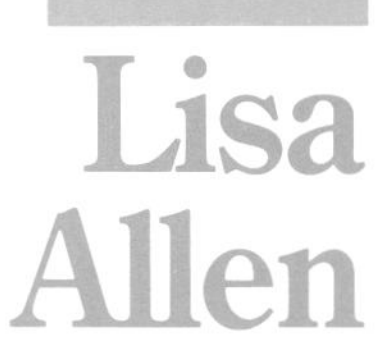

Lisa Allen

No one can fault Lisa Allen for timidity. She plunges into the maelstrom of paint with all the wanton abandon of a zealot. She works intuitively, without plan or calculation, trusting her instincts. Her art is a succession of improvisations, one *event* prompting another, each response further clarifying her intention. But such clarity is hard won. Allen's images are wrought, pulled forcibly out of the dense material. In the process she may radically and repeatedly alter a composition, testing all possibilities. The scarred surfaces of her paintings reveal the extremity of the struggle: whole passages may be scraped away or overlaid with sweeps of thick color. The struggle ends only when the artist snatches a moment's brief order out of the tumult. One is struck by the irony of the artist as her own adversary, striving to master the chaos of her own making.

J.W.C.

Born 1955 in Pekin, Illinois
Education: University of Illinois at Champaign-Urbana; B.F.A., 1977; M.F.A., 1979
Residence: Portland, Maine
Current position: Associate Professor, Portland School of Art, Portland, Maine

Selected Individual Exhibitions
1985 Art Gallery, University of Maine, Orono, Maine

1981 Artemisia Gallery, Chicago, Illinois

Selected Group Exhibitions
1987 Stephen Rosenberg Gallery, New York, New York

Maine Coast Artists Gallery, Rockport, Maine, *Maine Teachers*

1986 Hobe Sound Galleries North, Portland, Maine, *Maine Biennial Invitational*

1984 Portland Museum of Art, Portland, Maine, *Maine Drawing Biennial*

1983 Colby College Museum of Art, Waterville, Maine, *1983 Maine Biennial*

1982 Roswell Museum and Art Center, Roswell, New Mexico, *Fall Invitational*

Bowdoin College Museum of Art, Brunswick, Maine, *1982 Maine Artists Invitational*

Selected Bibliography
1986 Edgar Allen Beem. "Among New England's Best." *Maine Times,* November 21, 1986, pp. 1B-7B.

1982 Philip Isaacson. "Modern Maine Art: The Best and Brightest." *Maine Sunday Telegram,* August 22, 1982, p. 30A.

Edgar Allen Beem. "Finding Unity in the Bizarre at the Maine Festival." *Maine Times,* July 30, 1982, pp. 38-39.

Selected Fellowships and Awards
1987 Residency Fellowship, Roswell Museum and Art Center, Roswell, New Mexico

1983 Fellowship, National Endowment for the Arts

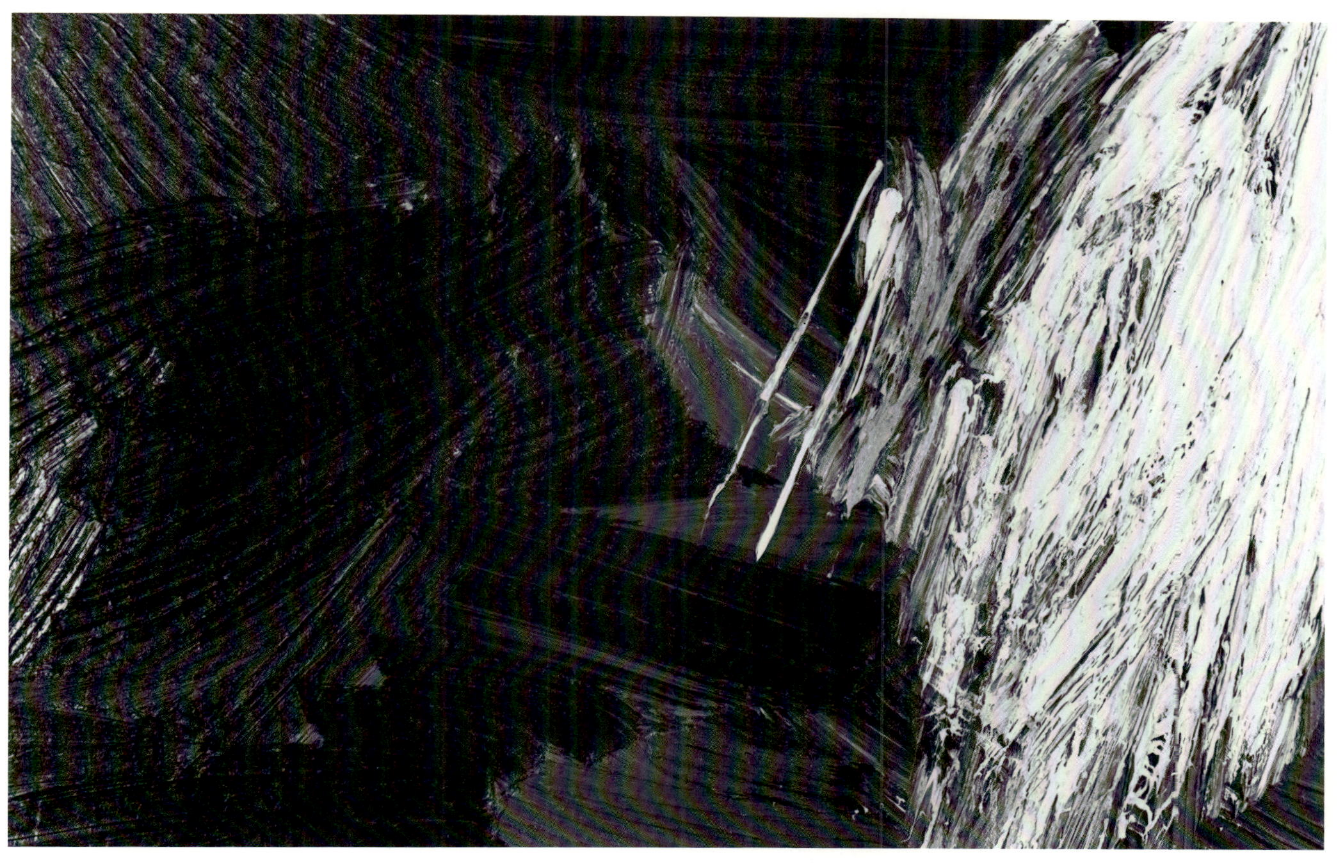

* *Willow,* 1986-87
oil, oil stick, and casein on panel
48 x 72 inches
Courtesy of Stephen Rosenberg Gallery,
New York, New York

Square Wheel, 1987
casein, graphite, oil stick,
and charcoal on paper
30 x 45 inches
Courtesy of Stephen Rosenberg Gallery

James Aponovich

With either brush or pencil in hand, Aponovich works within a sensitivity which stresses the beauty in physical substance. The tonalities of his drawings reveal indigenous harmonies and a heightened awareness of surface, texture, and form. The drawings and paintings display very delicate nuances of shape, color, and feeling in apparently factual appearances, or they may glow with the intensity of color. Every aspect of every image is presented as natural, without the least allusion to distortion and exaggeration. Aponovich does not simply make pictures about an environment familiar to himself and others. He draws and paints in order to isolate and describe the discovered qualities of the subject that appeal to his realization of the sensations inherent to their nature. His attention to detail, his delicacy of touch, and his use of vibrant color are indications that he is an artist in complete command of his work. His art is one of extremes, traversing the range between the real and the illusory, but always directed toward the goal of "getting at the particularness of anything I paint."

R.M.D.

Born 1948 in Nashua, New Hampshire
Education: University of New Hampshire,
Durham, New Hampshire; B.A., 1971
Residence: Nashua, New Hampshire

Selected Individual Exhibitions

1985-1987 Robert Schoelkopf Gallery, New York, New York

1985 The Currier Gallery of Art, Manchester, New Hampshire (traveling exhibition)

1982 The Alpha Gallery, Boston, Massachusetts

1981 The Sharon Arts Center, Sharon, New Hampshire

1979 The Currier Gallery of Art, Manchester, New Hampshire

1977 Chapel Art Center, Saint Anselm College, Manchester, New Hampshire

1976 New England College, Henniker, New Hampshire

Selected Group Exhibitions

1986 The Hudson River Museum, Yonkers, New York, *Form or Formula: Drawing and Drawings*

1985 San Francisco Museum of Modern Art, San Francisco, California, *American Realism: Twentieth-Century Drawings and Watercolors*

1984 Robert Schoelkopf Gallery, New York, New York, *Recent American Still Life Painting*

1984 Barbara Fendrick Gallery, Washington, D.C., *The Still Life*

1983 The Pennsylvania Academy of the Fine Arts, Philadelphia, Pennsylvania, *Perspectives on Contemporary American Realism*

1979, 1976, 1974 DeCordova and Dana Museum and Park, Lincoln, Massachusetts, *New England Drawing Competition*

Selected Bibliography

1985 Christine Gardner. "James Aponovich." *American Artist* 49 (November 1985), pp. 60-65, 104-110.

Selected Fellowships and Awards

1983, 1981 Artist Grant, New Hampshire Commission on the Arts

1976 Fellowship, National Endowment for the Arts

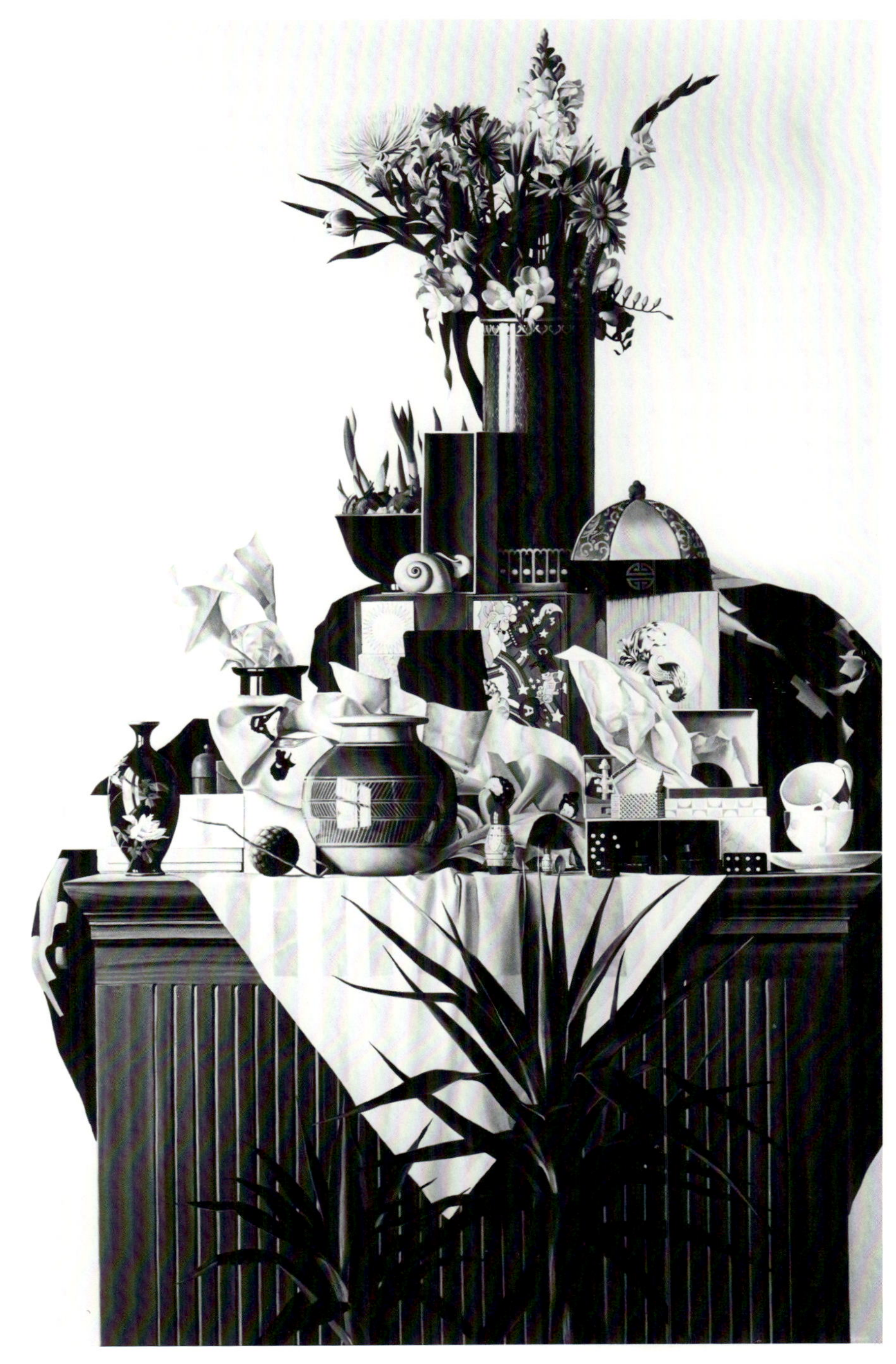

* *Still Life with Dominos,* 1987
oil on canvas
80 x 50 inches
Collection of Charles H. Howard III

Mary A. Armstrong

Mary Armstrong's recent paintings are embodiments of nature. Shimmering interpretations of water, flowers, and other natural forms, these paintings are inspired in format and mood by Italian trecento paintings. Yet, the imagery is completely of Armstrong's own invention; her paintings are translations of her feelings and responses to particular situations.

Painted on board, relatively small, and rendered primarily in delicate pinks and blues, Armstrong's paintings are iconic in their "objectness" and reverential intensity. The emphasis is on surface and the quality of light, rather than on space. Palette sticks, knives, fingertips, and rags for burnishing are used to create a rich, iridescent surface. Her work has always been characterized by overall patterning. In the newer paintings the patterning is seen in the increasingly abstracted shapes of the water, flowers, and fish, whose stylized forms become interchangeable.

In *Death in Summer: Bluefish*, her most recent painting in the exhibition, the red color resulted from the artist's deliberate effort to introduce earth colors into her palette. The image was triggered by Armstrong's strong reaction to seeing a bluefish in its death throes. The peaked, triangular "wave" shapes that she used to use for water refer here to the gills of the fish. Yet, without the title as a guide, what one sees is a mountain erupting, its red flames bloodlike. *Death in Summer* epitomizes the transformational qualities of Armstrong's paintings.

R.R.L.

Born 1948 in Torrington, Connecticut
Education: Skowhegan School of Painting and Sculpture, Skowhegan, Maine; 1977 Lesley College, Cambridge, Massachusetts; M.Ed., 1976 Boston University School of Visual Arts, Boston, Massachusetts; B.F.A., 1972 Residence: East Boston, Massachusetts Current position: Art teacher, Charles River School, Dover, Massachusetts

Selected Individual Exhibitions
1987, 1985 Victoria Munroe Gallery, New York, New York

1981 Impressions Gallery, Boston, Massachusetts

1980 Hudson D. Walker Gallery, Provincetown, Massachusetts

Selected Group Exhibitions
1986 Leo Castelli Gallery, New York, New York, *Skowhegan: A Ten-Year Retrospective 1975-1985* (traveling exhibition)

Victoria Munroe Gallery, *Painters on Paper*

Summit Art Center, Summit, New Jersey, *Objects Observed*

Metropolitan Museum and Art Center, Coral Gables, Florida, *Fifty Works: Selections from the E.F. Hutton Collection*

The Picker Art Gallery, Colgate University, Hamilton, New York, *Gender and Gesture*

1984 DeCordova and Dana Museum and Park, Lincoln, Massachusetts, *Contemporary New England Still Life* (traveling exhibition)

1980 Institute of Contemporary Art, Boston, Massachusetts, *Seven Graphic Artists*

Selected Bibliography
1985 Grace Glueck. "Art: Narrative Works with a Latin Twist." *New York Times,* April 12, 1985, p. C20.

Charles Guiliano. "Six Neo-Romantic Artists." *Art New England* 3 (April 1985), p. 11.

Christine Temin. "Romantic Landscapes from Six Bay Staters." *Boston Globe,* February 21, 1985, p. 69.

1984 Charles Guiliano. "Exhibits May Vary, but Quality Doesn't." *Patriot Ledger* (Quincy, Massachusetts), February 19, 1984.

Judy Goldman. "Contemporary New England Still Life." *Art New England* 5 (December 1984), p. 12.

Robert Taylor. "DeCordova Presents a Variety of Still Life." *Boston Globe,* October 7, 1984, p. 77.

1981 Christine Temin. "Romance in the Tea Bowls," *Boston Globe,* September 17, 1981.

Selected Fellowships and Awards
1981 The Blanche Coleman Award in Painting, Boston, Massachusetts

1980 Fellowship, The Artists Foundation, Boston, Massachusetts

1979-81 Fellowship, The Fine Arts Work Center, Provincetown, Massachusetts

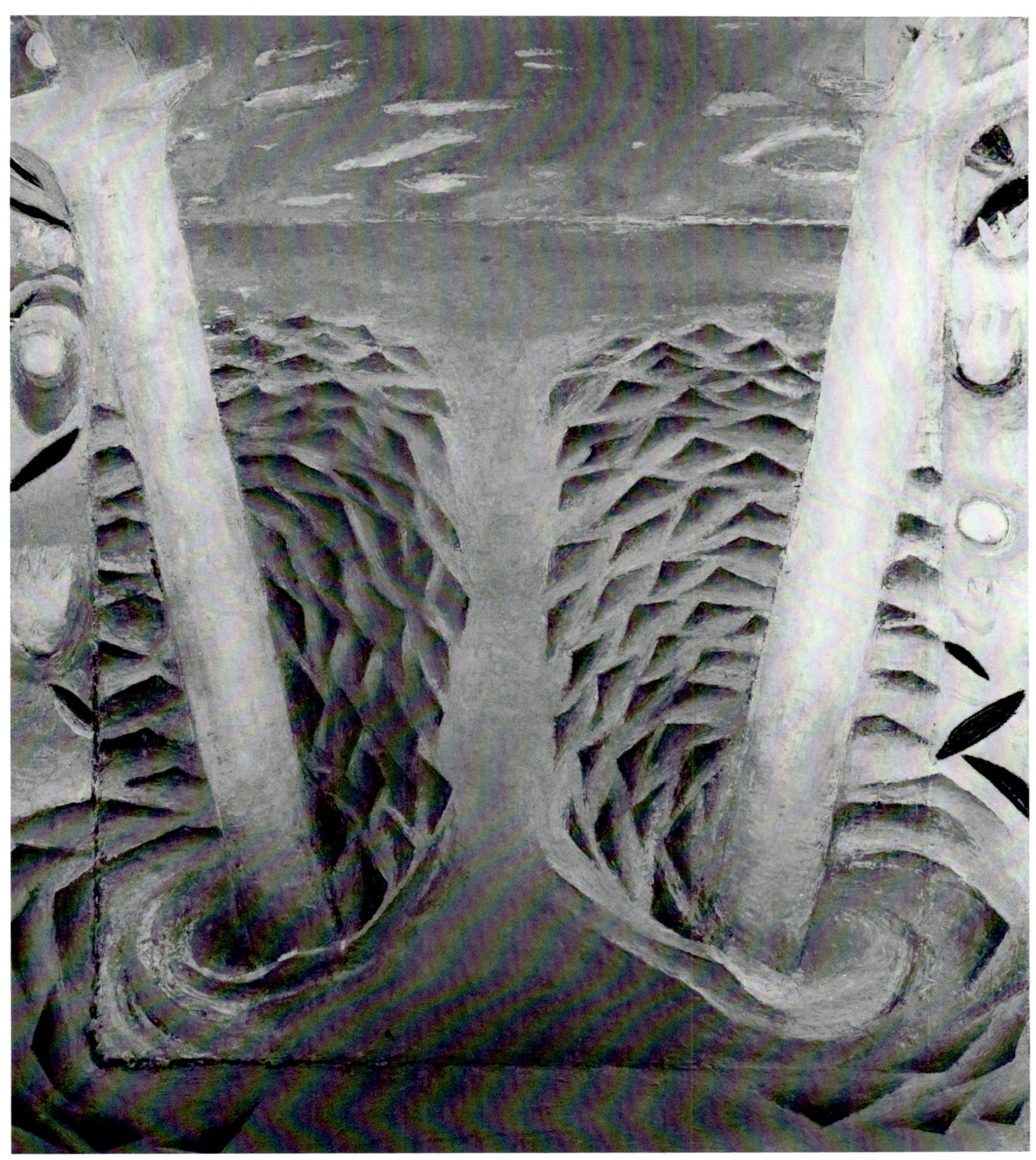

* *What Our Dreams Will Give Us,* 1985-86
oil on panel
34 x 29½ inches
Courtesy of Victoria Munroe Gallery

Summer Song: Endangered Species, 1986
oil on panel
30¼ x 23½ inches
Courtesy of Victoria Munroe Gallery,
New York, New York

Death in Summer: Bluefish, 1987
oil on panel
32 x 27¾ inches
Courtesy of Victoria Munroe Gallery

Howard Ben Tré

Howard Ben Tré's meeting with glass artist Dale Chihuly in Portland, Oregon, in 1976 was decisive, not only in Ben Tré's choice of glass as a medium but in his move to Providence to attend the Rhode Island School of Design. Inspired by Chihuly's energy level but not interested in glass blowing, Ben Tré began to cast glass using a process based on the metal casting which had fascinated him since his high school days. Glass is an important aspect of his work, allowing him to take heavy, dense objects, move them out of their "literalness," and draw other references and associations from them.

The sculptures are grounded in the artist's continuing study of architectural history. From his first castings, based on the floor plans of pre-Renaissance churches and Mayan ziggurats, through the Providence pieces, which reflected the city's prominent position during the industrial revolution, to the columns, which portray either the soaring spirituality and verticality of a medieval abbey or the downward pressure exerted by enormous Greek capitals, the work transforms architectural elements from the past into ceremonial objects for the twentieth century.

The latest works, based on freeways, lintels, and bridges, transcend their engineered prototypes and, with the addition of metallic elements, afford the viewer a ritualistic experience.

N.R.V.

Born 1949 in Brooklyn, New York
Education: Rhode Island School of
Design, Providence, Rhode Island;
M.F.A., 1980
Portland State University, Portland,
Oregon; B.S.A., 1978
Residence: Providence, Rhode Island

Selected Individual Exhibitions
1987 Fay Gold Gallery, Atlanta, Georgia

1986 John Berggruen Gallery, San Francisco, California

1985 Charles Cowles Gallery, New York, New York

1985, 1983, 1981 Habatat Galleries, Detroit, Michigan

1985, 1983, 1981, 1980 Hadler/Rodriguez Galleries, Houston, Texas

1983 Clark Gallery, Lincoln, Massachusetts

1983, 1981 Foster/White Gallery, Seattle, Washington

Selected Group Exhibitions
1987 University Art Museum, Arizona State University, Tempe, Arizona, *3 + 3 x 7, Sculpture in Glass and Works on Paper*

1986 The Saint Louis Art Museum, St. Louis, Missouri, *Art of the 80s*

Rose Art Museum, Brandeis University, Waltham, Massachusetts, *Sculptural Objects and Installations*

John Berggruen Gallery, San Francisco, California, *Sculpture and Works in Relief*

Charles Cowles Gallery, New York, New York, *The Heroic Sublime*

American Craft Museum, New York, New York, *Poetry of the Physical*

1985 The Detroit Institute of Arts, Detroit, Michigan, *Detroit Collects*

Selected Bibliography
1987 Donald Kuspit. *High Glass Art.* Visual Arts Center, California State University, Fullerton, California.

1986 Michael Brenson. "A Fall Art Scene that's Bristling with Energy: Genteel SoHo Is Still a Vital Center of Activity." *New York Times,* November 7, 1986, p. C26.

1985 Grace Glueck. "Art: Narrative Works with a Latin Twist." *New York Times,* April 12, 1985, p. C20.

1983 Barbara Jepson. "This Sculptor's World Is Made of Glass." *Wall Street Journal,* November 9, 1983, p. 28

1982 Kenneth Baker. "Howard Ben Tré." *Arts Magazine* 57 (September 1982), p. 8.

Todd Brewster. "Avant Glass." *Life Magazine* 5 no. 2 (February 1982), p. 78.

1980 Ronald J. Onorato. "Howard Ben Tré." *Arts Magazine* 54 (June 1980), p. 5.

Selected Fellowships and Awards
1987 Rakow Award, The Corning Museum of Glass, Corning, New York

1984, 1980 Fellowship, National Endowment for the Arts

1984, 1979 Individual Artist's Fellowship, Rhode Island State Council on the Arts

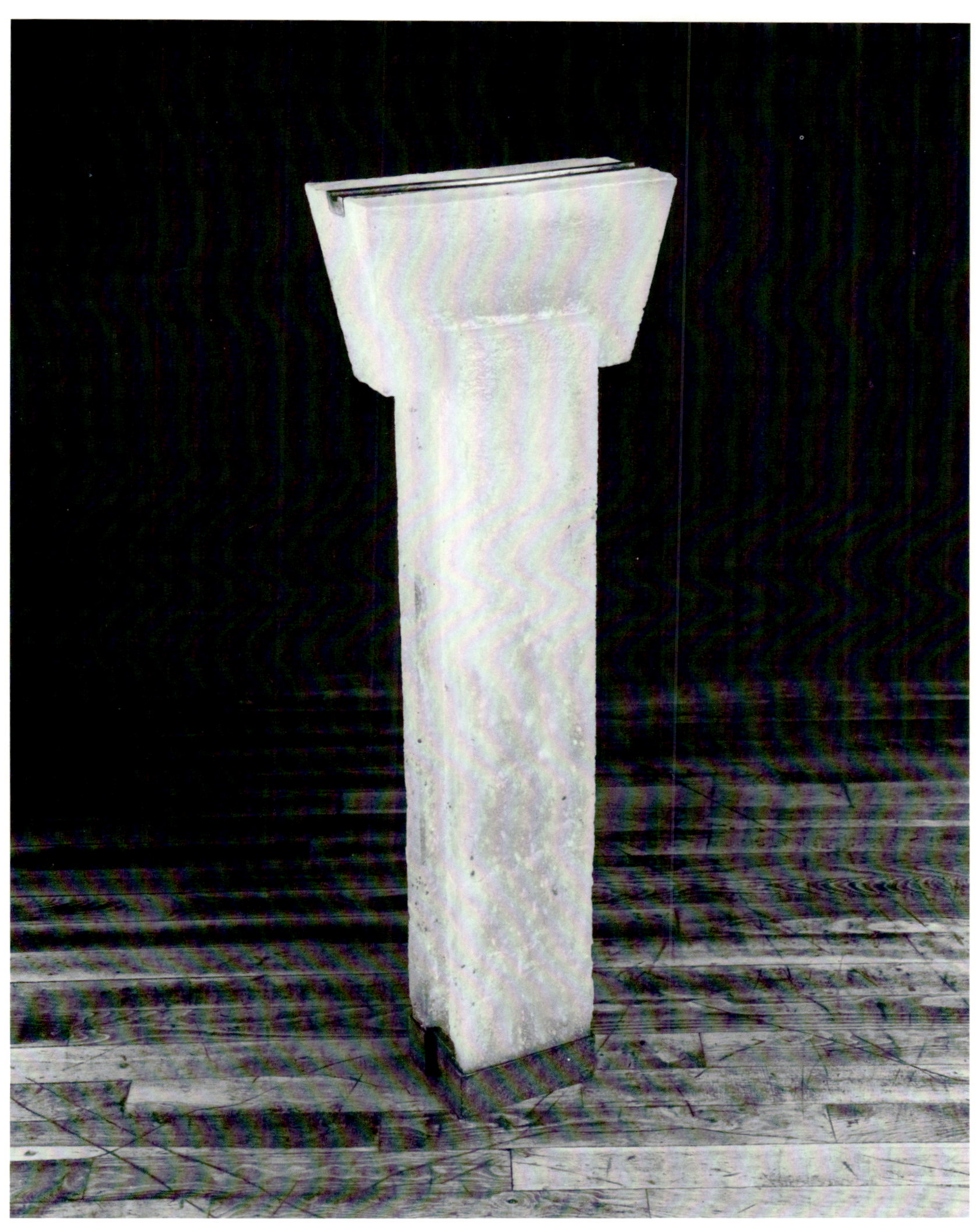

* *Dedicant #3,* 1986
glass, patinated brass, lead, and gold leaf
49 x 16¼ x 7¼ inches
Lent by Charles Cowles Gallery,
New York, New York

Varujan Boghosian

Reviewing for *The New York Times,* John Russell wrote, "Varujan Boghosian is well known by now as a master of the low-relief construction. In these constructions he functions both as a monumental mason, who in another age could have built one of the smaller Pyramids, and as a poet with his own ideas about human beauty and the vicissitudes to which life can subject it." In both his constructions and collages, there is a strong sense of personal, introspective history.

Aged materials are carefully selected and juxtaposed to evoke the realms of myth and mystery. The objects incorporated in each work are steeped in associations with the past, a yearning for time lost which is expressed in icons for the present. Boghosian is fascinated by all sorts of special materials, which he uses with wit and elegance to set up puzzles, surprises, and conflicts over the original nature and purpose of the various elements included in his works. His work is a matter of exploring identity and, through identity, charting shifts in meanings. He deftly aligns and unites items and materials which were originally made for some entirely different purpose and have been discarded by others as being exhausted. These souvenirs, collected by a traveler, are placed in new combinations, allowing him to test how far a meaning may be taken in each work and to what extent the items must be modified, or rearranged in new combinations, before a meaning shifts into an area of heightened ambiguity, opening the way for communication of new significance.

R.M.D.

Born 1926 in New Britain, Connecticut
Education: Yale University School of Art
and Architecture, New Haven,
Connecticut; M.F.A., 1959
Yale University, New Haven,
Connecticut; B.F.A., 1957
Residence: Hanover, New Hampshire
Current position: George Frederick
Jewett Professor of Art, Dartmouth
College

Selected Individual Exhibitions
1987 Cordier & Ekstrom, New York, New York. Periodic exhibitions since 1969

Bucknell University, Lewisburg, Pennsylvania

Boston Public Library, Boston, Massachusetts

1986 American Academy, Rome

1970 The Arts Club of Chicago, Chicago, Illinois

1968 Hopkins Center, Dartmouth College, Hanover, New Hampshire (traveling exhibition)

1966 The Stable Gallery, New York, New York. Periodic exhibitions since 1963.

Selected Group Exhibitions
1987 Longpoint Gallery, Provincetown, Massachusetts. Annual exhibitions since 1981.

1968, 1966, 1964, 1962, 1960 Whitney Museum of American Art, New York, New York, *Annual Exhibition.*

1966 The Hanover Gallery, London, England, *The Poetic Image*

The Institute of Contemporary Art, Boston, Massachusetts, *The Found Object*

1964 The New School, New York, New York, *The Artist's Reality: An International Sculpture Exhibition*

1961 Krannert Art Museum, University of Illinois, Urbana, Illinois, *Contemporary American Painting and Sculpture*

1956 The Museum of Modern Art, New York, New York, *Recent Drawings USA*

Selected Fellowships and Awards
1985 Fellowship, John Simon Guggenheim Memorial Foundation

1975, 1966-67 Sculptor in Residence, American Academy in Rome

1972 Award, National Institute of Arts and Letters

1968 Artist in Residence, Dartmouth College, Hanover, New Hampshire

1966 Fellowship, Howard Foundation

1961 Specialist's Grant, United States Department of State

1953 Fulbright Fellowship

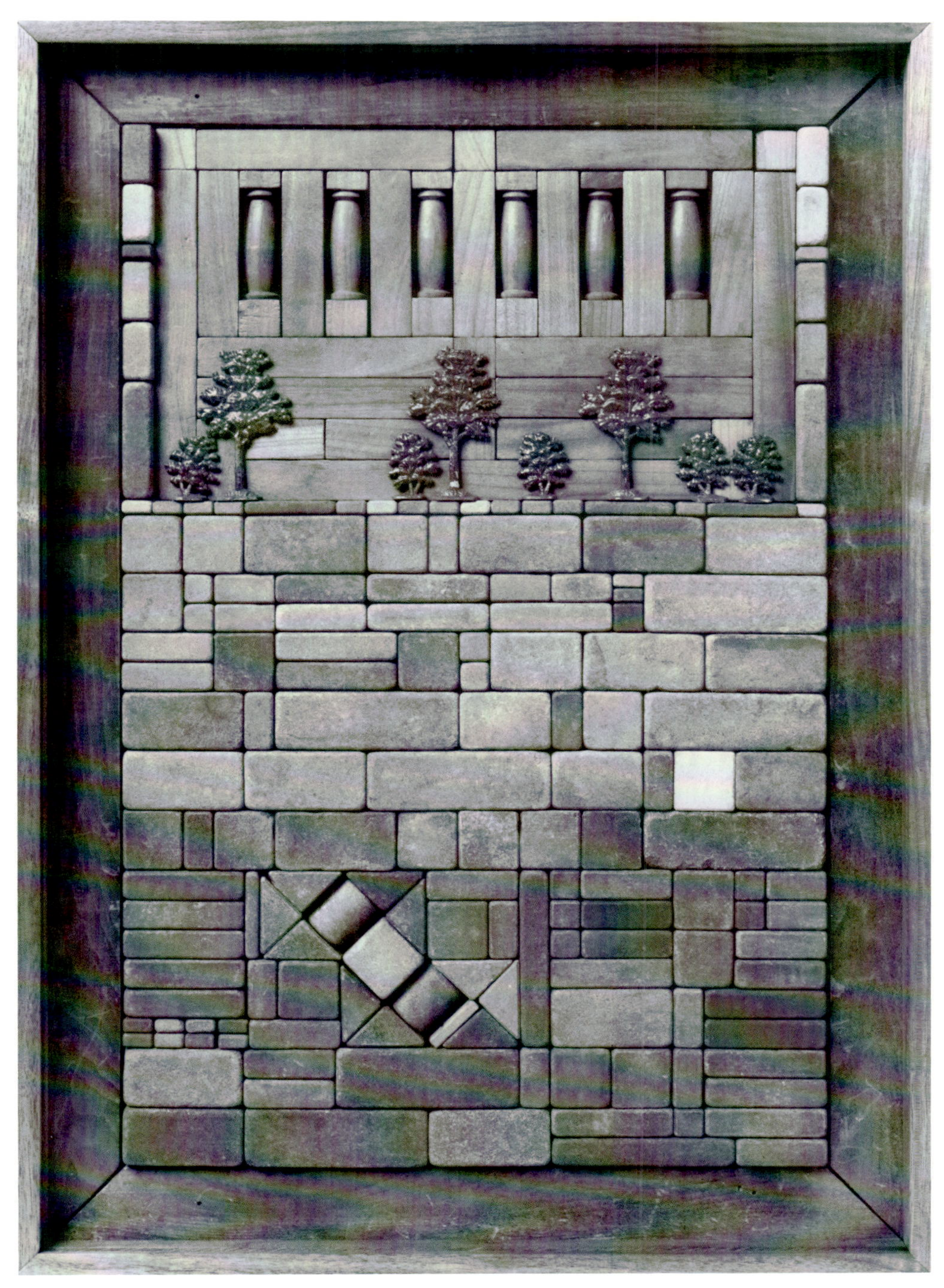

* *Grecian Landscape,* 1987
mixed media construction
24 x 16 inches
Lent by the artist

Eleanor Briggs

Emile Zola's observation that: "A work of art is a detail of nature seen through a temperament" is well proven in the work of Eleanor Briggs. She functions as a mediator between the audience and the environment, exploiting a special ability to detect the characteristics which remain hidden, but available, within most settings and happenings. Her images are distinguished by a difference in viewpoint, a firm understanding of the subtle changes of light and its power to define form or to indicate the passage of time. Even the momentary and transient are given form; the unknown becomes known as she gathers enough precisely balanced elements to make each image a self-contained entity. Perception, sensitivity, and imagination are all essential for the transformation of the commonplace. The camera is the least important of all the elements which must harmonize in order to document the elusive and ineffable. Her photographs do not broadcast messages but rather offer the opportunity to go beyond the limitations of the human mind by provoking new responses. Firmly in command of the camera's potential, and continually searching for new content, Eleanor Briggs demonstrates, in her work, a sensibility far beyond the common ability to perceive.

R.M.D.

Born 1939 in New York, New York
Education: Sweet Briar College,
Sweet Briar, Virginia; B.A., 1961
Residence: Hancock, New Hampshire

Selected Individual Exhibitions
1987 Chapel Art Center, Saint Anselm College, Manchester, New Hampshire

1984 The Currier Gallery of Art, Manchester, New Hampshire

1982 Photography Gallery, Sanibel, Florida

1981 Hopkins Center, Dartmouth College, Hanover, New Hampshire

1979 AVA Gallery, Hanover, New Hampshire

1978 Saint Botolph Club, Boston, Massachusetts

Selected Group Exhibitions
1986 Sharon Arts Center, Sharon, New Hampshire, *Photographic Insights*

Hood Museum of Art, Dartmouth College, Hanover, New Hampshire, *Regional Selections*

1985 The Currier Gallery of Art, Manchester, New Hampshire, *The Photographer, the Portrait, and the Environment*

Colby-Sawyer College, New London, New Hampshire, *Four Photographers*

1983 The Currier Gallery of Art, Manchester, New Hampshire, *New Hampshire Art Association: Thirty-seventh Annual Exhibition*

Saint-Gaudens National Historic Site, Cornish, New Hampshire, *Graphics/New Hampshire*

1979 Philadelphia Print Club, Philadelphia, Pennsylvania, *Annual Exhibition*

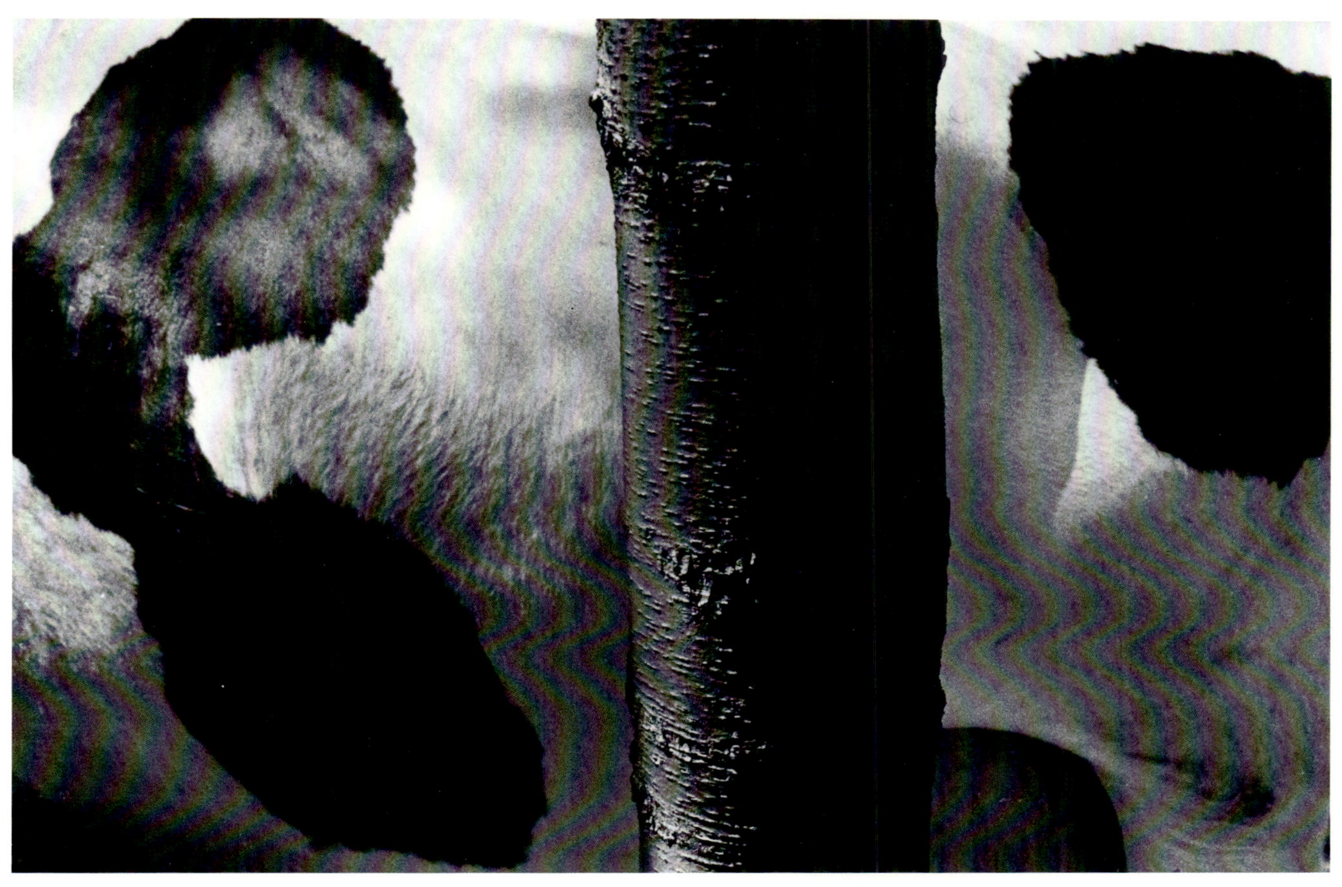

* *Cowscape Series,* 1984
five photographs
each image: 11 x 14 inches
Lent by the artist

Malcolm Cochran

Cochran's constructions bridge a gap between traditional ideas of sculpture and architecture, arriving at a new manifestation of both. The work is based on a strong regard for human values, expressed through grand objects made from fragments of New England architecture and artifacts. A sense of history and memories of time past pervade his work. *Bedroom* (1978) commemorated the life of a man who lived alone by recreating a reference to his house and its contents. Other works, such as *Dream of Arcadia* (Artpark 1981) and *Chapels of Ease* (Art Festival of Atlanta 1984), take their inspiration from nineteenth-century architecture which has been changed by time and nature. In all his pieces, he juxtaposes salvaged material and objects, which take on new meanings and associations, developing a narrative about the aura and prevalence of the human spirit. His pieces have a very intense, physical reality, with traces and suggestions of a humanity which transforms all that it touches. Mystery and ambiguity are central to Cochran's intentions, effects reached through consistent attention to craft and workmanship. He explores the relationship between dreams and objective experience, reality and substance, calling upon associations and cues which unlock private emotions and recall events which shaped private destinies.

R.M.D.

Born 1948 in New London,
New Hampshire
Education: Cranbrook Academy of Art,
Bloomfield Hills, Michigan; M.F.A., 1973
Wesleyan University, Middletown,
Connecticut; B.A., 1971
Residence: Sutton Mills, New Hampshire
Current position: Associate Professor
of Art, Ohio State University

Selected Individual Exhibitions
1984, 1980 The Currier Gallery of Art, Manchester, New Hampshire

1978 Greenville County Museum of Art, Greenville, South Carolina

1977 Dartmouth College Museum and Galleries, Hanover, New Hampshire

Selected Group Exhibitions
1987 University Gallery of Fine Art, Ohio State University, Columbus, Ohio, *Visiting Artists Show*

1986 Chautauqua Art Association Galleries, Chautauqua Institution, Chautauqua, New York, *School of Art Faculty Show*

1984 Brattleboro Museum & Art Center, Brattleboro, Vermont, *WORKS of Art*

Art Festival of Atlanta, Atlanta, Georgia, *Chapels of Ease*

1981 The Currier Gallery of Art, Manchester, New Hampshire, *Sculpture: New Hampshire*

Artpark, Lewiston, New York, *Dream of Arcadia*

1980 The Copley Society, Boston, *The Mood of New England, Past and Present*

Selected Fellowships and Awards
1986 Artist Grant, New Hampshire Council on the Arts

1985 Art in Public Places Grant, National Endowment for the Arts

1983 Fellowship, National Endowment for the Arts

1980 Artist in Residence Grant, National Endowment for the Arts

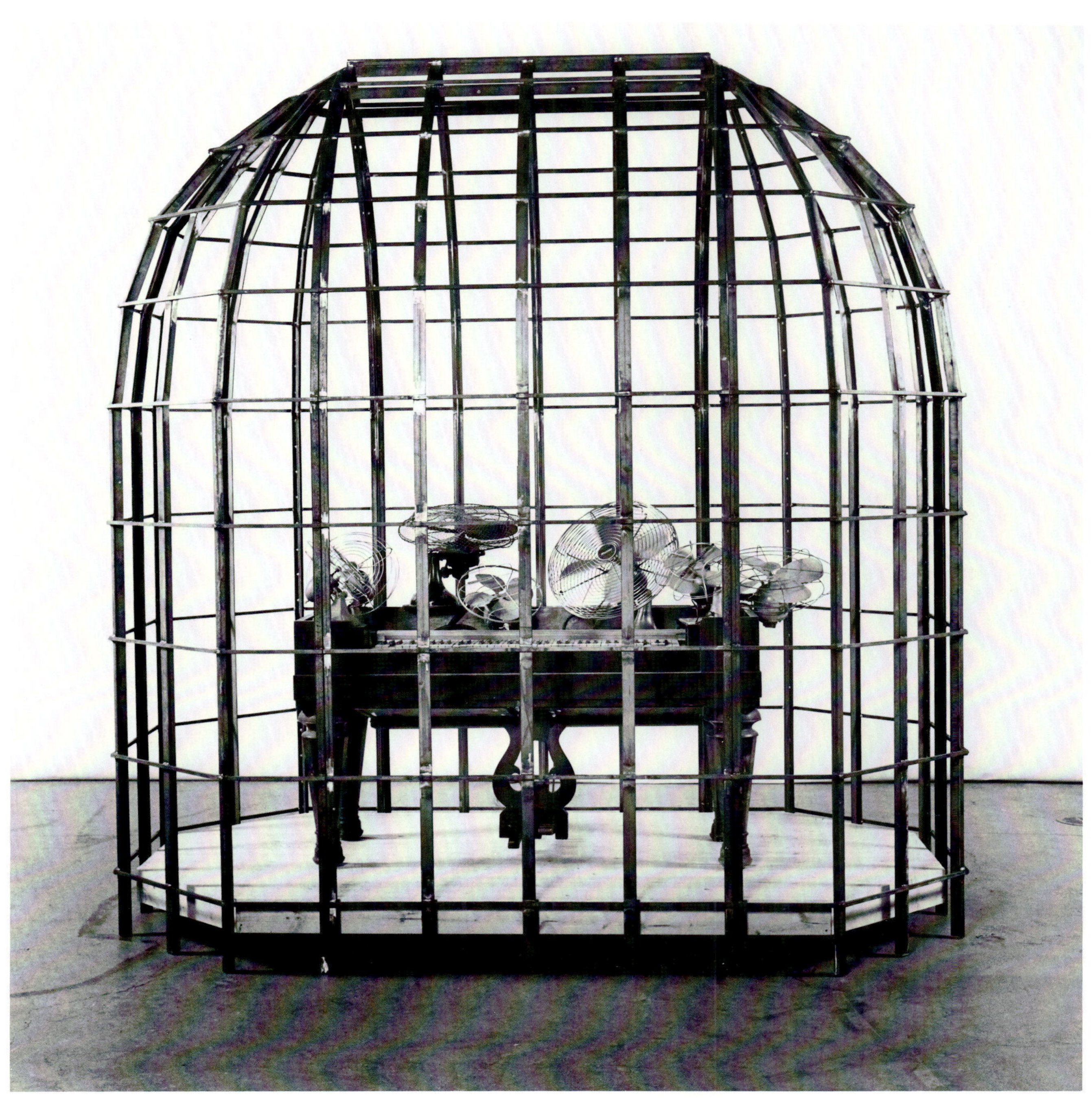

*   *Song Without Words (for Amy Beech),* 1987
mixed media
108 x 108 x 60 inches
Lent by the artist

Robert Ferrandini

Water and sky play prominent roles in all of Ferrandini's paintings. Though often based on specific places, his buildings and land- and seascapes are flavored with a strong dose of the imaginary.

Ferrandini paints on paper with oil, building up a luminous surface with layers of brushstrokes. The romanticism in his work is perhaps most evident in his paintings of turbulent seas and expressive skies but is also present in the more peaceful, lyrical paintings. He imbues the landscape of late twentieth-century Boston with a late nineteenth-century quality of the sublime, while adding his own sense of impending disaster.

The fantastic images of *All Creatures Great and Small* derive in part from Ferrandini's interest in science fiction and comic books. In this painting, a whale, a sea serpent, other fanciful animals, and the prow of a boat crest in a gigantic wave along with a building and a tree that has been uprooted. Flat-topped buildings and delicate feathery trees are Ferrandini trademarks, representing man's two environments, the man-made and the natural.

Ferrandini's recent work alternates between calm, poetic references to specific places or sources of inspiration and catastrophic images in which the world appears close to destruction. The sense of humor with which they are painted and their sheer beauty dispel the initial feeling of terror.

R.R.L.

Born 1948 in Boston, Massachusetts
Education: Massachusetts College of Art, Boston, Massachusetts; B.F.A., 1972; M.F.A., 1973
California Institute for the Arts, Valencia, California, 1972
Residence: Winthrop, Massachusetts

Selected Individual Exhibitions
1987 Sette Gallery, Scottsdale, Arizona

1987, 1984 Stavaridis Gallery, Boston, Massachusetts

1986 Victoria Munroe Gallery, New York, New York

1983 Impressions Gallery, Boston, Massachusetts

1980 Provincetown Group Gallery, Provincetown, Massachusetts

Selected Group Exhibitions
1986 Miami-Dade Community College, Miami, Florida, *Black and White Prevails: A Selection of Contemporary Drawings*

Massachusetts College of Art, Boston, Massachusetts, *Insights*

1985 Mount Holyoke College Art Museum, South Hadley, Massachusetts, *An Architect's Eye: Selections from the Collection of Graham Gund*

Boston College, Chestnut Hill, Massachusetts, *Group Show*

1984 Victoria Munroe Gallery, New York, New York, *A Sense of Place*

1982 Institute of Contemporary Art, Boston, Massachusetts, *Boston Now: Figuration*

1980 DeCordova and Dana Museum and Park, Lincoln, Massachusetts, *The DeCordova/Three Decades*

Selected Bibliography
1987 David Bonetti. "Robert Ferrandini." *Artnews* 86 (Summer 1987), p. 60.

David Bonetti. "On and Off the Street. Local Color, Local Landscape, Local... ." *Boston Phoenix,* March 24, 1987, p. 4.

Christine Temin. "Sticking with Established Recognizable Style." *Boston Globe,* March 5, 1987, p. 86.

1986 Norman Keyes. "Tracing the Careers of Six Boston Artists." *Boston Globe,* September 8, 1986, p. 88.

1985 Christine Temin. "Romantic Landscapes from Six Bay Staters." *Boston Globe,* February 21, 1985, p. 69.

1983 Rebecca Nemser. "Robert Ferrandini." *Art New England* 4 (April 1983).

Kenneth Baker. "Robert Ferrandini's No-Fault Lines." *Boston Phoenix,* May 23, 1982, p. A42.

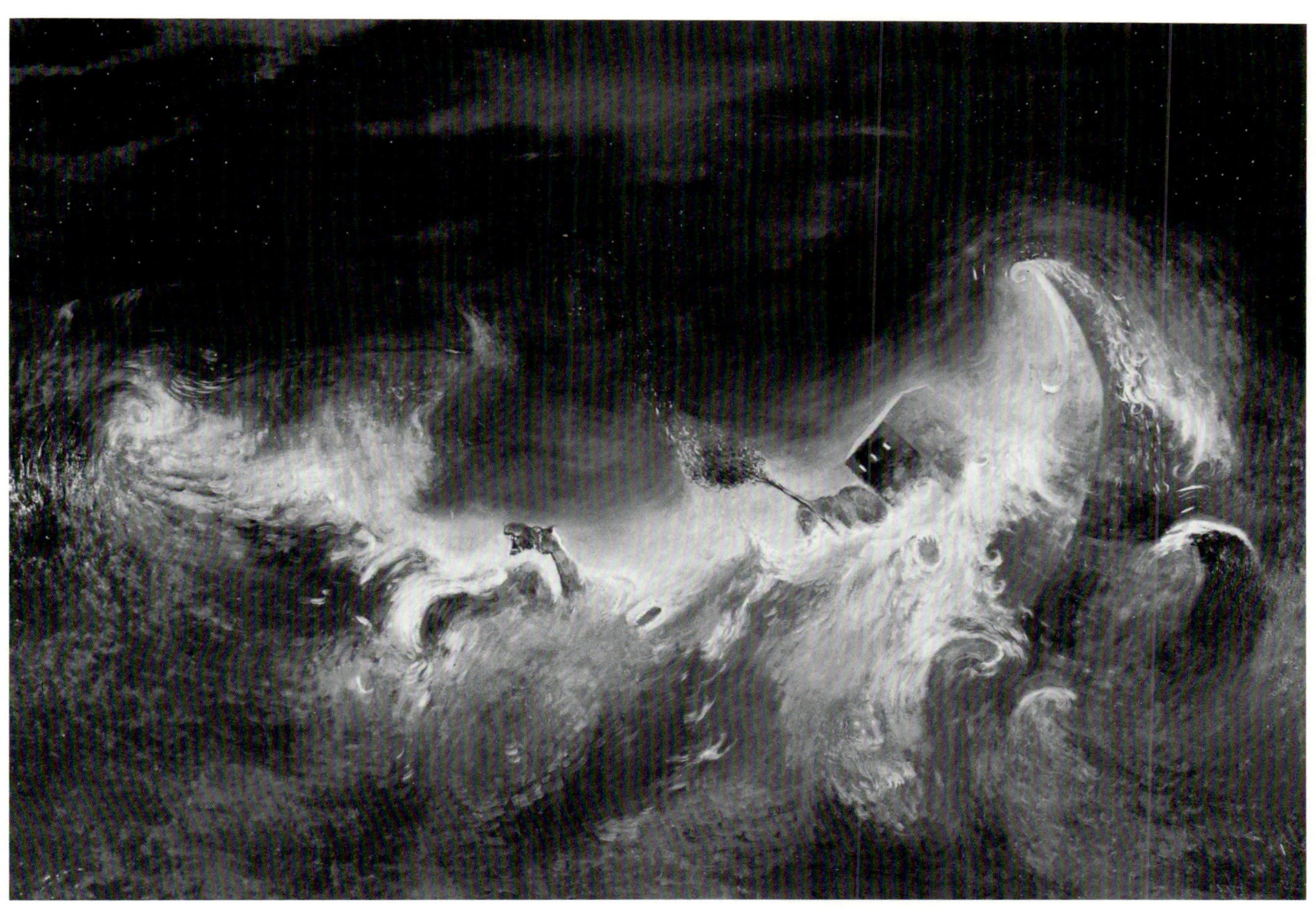

* *All Creatures Great and Small,* 1987
oil on paper
28½ x 38½ inches
Private collection

Untitled (View of Boston), 1986
oil on paper
28½ x 38½ inches
Collection Prudential-Bache

Gregory Gillespie

Gregory Gillespie's paintings radiate an intensified realism which allows us to see every hair on a person's face and every scratch on the surface of a wall. That same intensity carries the work beyond natural reality to an inner emotional and psychological reality and produces hallucinatory drawings whose distorted androgynous forms emerge entirely from the artist's imagination.

Portrait of Bella epitomizes the coexistence of fantasy and reality in Gillespie's work. His dealer, Bella Fishko, is seen in front of a wall covered with other Gillespie works. The artist appears in the painting as a Lilliputian, standing on a shelf pointing to a palette. The difference in scale with which the artist and the dealer are rendered symbolizes, perhaps, the nature of their relationship. Gillespie sees his dealer as a protector whose creativity lies in recognizing and nurturing talent and taking care of the business side of art.

Portrait of Bella contains references to all of Gillespie's artistic endeavors—portraiture, studio interiors, landscapes imbued with the Northern European tradition of old master paintings, and fantastic automatic drawings and prints. The latter aspect of Gillespie's work is represented in this exhibition by an untitled oil on paper in which male and female genitalia and primitive African figures converge in an erotic design.

The two apparently contradictory aspects of Gillespie's work—extreme realism and wild fantasy—are necessary components of the totality of the artist's vision. By combining them, he creates paintings and drawings that pulsate with a riveting intensity.

R.R.L.

Born 1936 in Roselle Park, New Jersey
Education: San Francisco Art Institute,
San Francisco, California; B.A., 1962;
M.F.A., 1962
Cooper Union for the Advancement of
Science and Art, New York, New York;
1954-1960
Residence: Belchertown, Massachusetts

Selected Individual Exhibitions

1987 Forum Gallery, New York, New York

1986 Duke University Museum of Art, Durham, North Carolina

1983 John Berggruen Gallery, San Francisco, California

1982 Alpha Gallery, Boston, Massachusetts

1977 Hirshhorn Museum and Sculpture Garden, Washington, D.C.

1971 Smith College Museum of Art, Northampton, Massachusetts

1969 American Academy, Rome, Italy

Selected Group Exhibitions

1986 Wichita Art Museum, Wichita, Kansas, *A Decade of American Realism: 1975-1985*

1984 Rose Art Museum, Brandeis University, Waltham, Massachusetts, *The Art of William Beckman and Gregory Gillespie* (traveling exhibition)

1983 University Art Museum, Santa Barbara, California, *A Heritage Renewed: Representational Drawing Today* (traveling exhibition)

Contemporary Arts Museum, Houston, Texas, *American Still Life: 1945-1983* (traveling exhibition)

1982 Whitney Museum of American Art, New York, New York, *Focus on the Figure: Twenty Years*

1981 The Pennsylvania Academy of the Fine Arts, Philadelphia, Pennsylvania, *Contemporary American Realism since 1960* (traveling exhibition)

1976 The American Academy and Institute of Arts and Letters, New York, New York, *Exhibition of Work by Newly Elected Members and Recipients of Honors and Awards*

Selected Bibliography

1986 David Bonetti. "On and Off the Street: Gregory Gillespie and Other Gallery Events." *Boston Phoenix,* April 15, 1986, p. 2.

Gerrit Henry. "Gregory Gillespie's Manic Masterpieces." *Artnews* 85 (December 1986), pp. 117-120.

1970 *Gregory Gillespie: Paintings (Italy 1962-1970).* Forum Gallery, 1970.

Selected Fellowships and Awards

1976 Academy-Institute Award in Art, National Academy of Arts and Letters

1972 Saltus Gold Medal for Merit, National Academy of Design

1967 Grant for Painting, Louis Comfort Tiffany Foundation

1964 Chester Dale Fellowship, American Academy, Rome, Italy

1963 Fulbright Fellowship

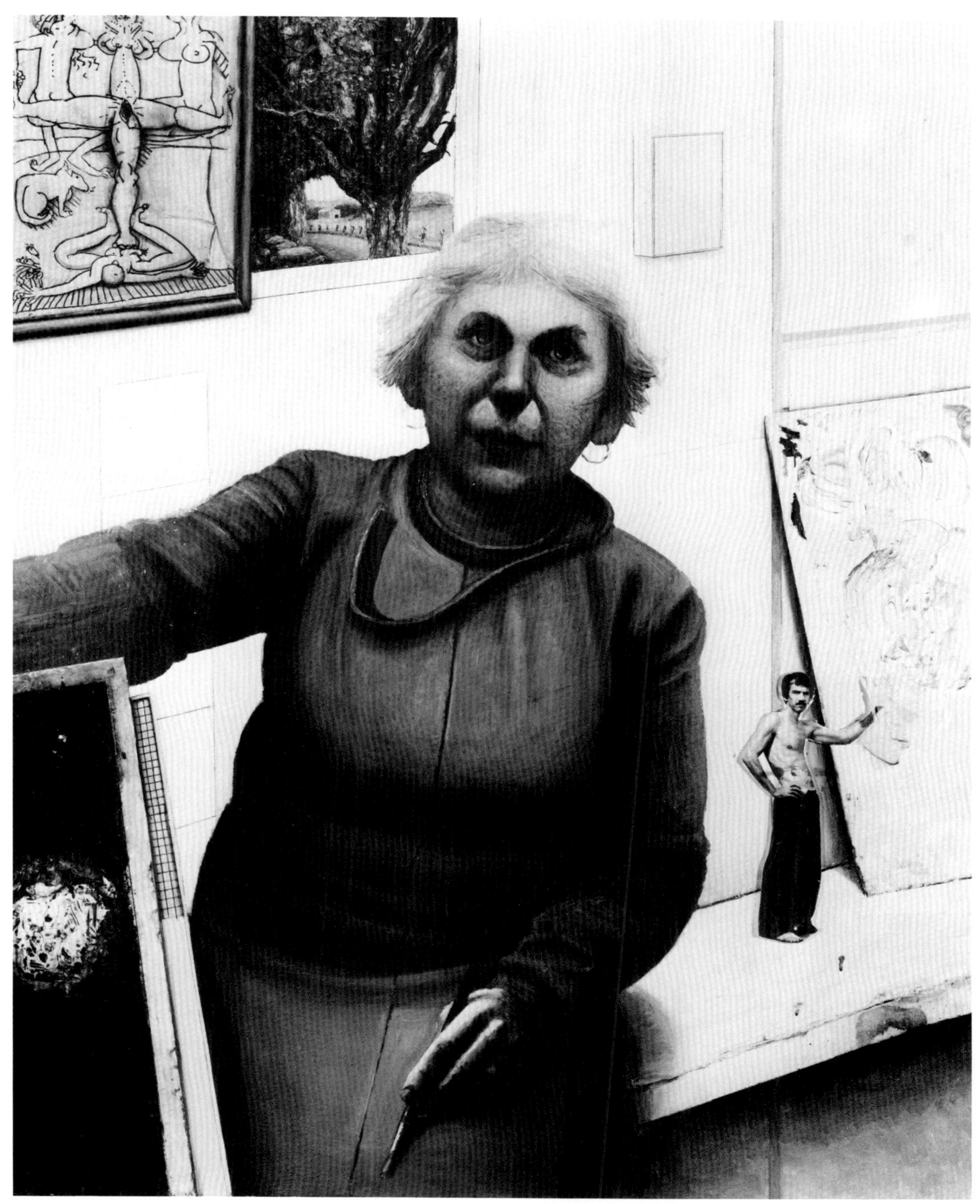

* *Portrait of Bella,* 1987
oil on alkyd on canvas on wood
48½ x 39 inches
Courtesy of Forum Gallery,
New York, New York

Sea Horse, 1987
oil on paper
26½ x 13 inches
Courtesy of Forum Gallery

James Grashow

James Grashow is a printmaker, sculptor, illustrator, and maker of environmental works. His woodcut prints appear regularly in *Time, The New York Times,* and *New York Magazine.* The laborious task of woodcutting demands tremendous discipline, which Grashow demonstrates in the extraordinary surfaces and attention to detail of his three-dimensional work.

A City is James Grashow's sixth environmental work, and, like the others, it takes as its underlying theme a humorous questioning of his subject matter. The room-sized metropolis of thirteen skyscrapers is composed of wood, cardboard, paint, paper, and cloth. Included in this show are four of the individual buildings which make up *A City.* Grashow wants *A City* to be "a walk-in painting." The intensity of the decoration, the almost compulsive surface patterning, and the anthropomorphic character of the buildings can give the viewer unending visual delights. Grashow wants the viewer to move among the individual buildings, not simply to look at them from outside an installation barrier.

D.C.D.

Born 1942 in Brooklyn, New York
Education: Pratt Institute, Brooklyn, New York; B.F.A., 1961; M.F.A, 1963
Residence: West Redding, Connecticut

Selected Individual Exhibitions
1987 North Carolina Museum of Art, Raleigh, North Carolina

Bucknell University Center Gallery, Lewisburg, Pennsylvania

1985 American Institute of Architects, Washington, D.C.

The New Britain Museum of American Art, New Britain, Connecticut

1984 Lamont Gallery, Phillips Exeter Academy, Exeter, New Hampshire

The Aldrich Museum of Contemporary Art, Ridgefield, Connecticut

Allan Stone Gallery, New York, New York. Periodic exhibitions since 1966.

Selected Group Exhibitions
1987 The Aldrich Museum of Contemporary Art, Ridgefield, Connecticut, *State of the Art*

1980 Society of Illustrators, Museum of American Illustration , New York, New York

Philadelphia Print Club, Philadelphia, Pennsylvania

1979 Associated American Artists, New York, New York

1974 The Clocktower, New York, New York

1972 The Hudson River Museum, Yonkers, New York

Selected Bibliography
1987 Barbara Cohen et al., eds. *New York Observed: Artists and Writers Look at the City, 1650 to the Present.* New York: Abrams, 1987.

Patrick Crean and Penney Kome, eds. *Peace: A Dream Unfolding.* San Francisco: Sierra Club, 1987.

1986 Steven Heller, *Innovators of American Illustration.* Van Nostrand Reinhold, 1986.

1982 J. Cottingham. "James Grashow: Prints and Sculpture." *American Artist* 46 (May 1982), pp. 70-75.

Steven Heller. "James Grashow." *Arts Magazine* 56 (June 1982), p. 12.

1981 Steven Heller. "James Grashow." *Graphics* 37 (1981/82), pp. 80-87.

1975 V. F. Brooks. "Trespassing on Wood, with Love." *Print* 29 (May 1975), pp. 57-65.

Selected Fellowships and Awards
1965 Grant for Graphics, Louis Comfort Tiffany Foundation

1964 Fellowship, Pratt Institute

1963 Grant for Painting and Graphics, Italian Government

Fulbright Fellowship

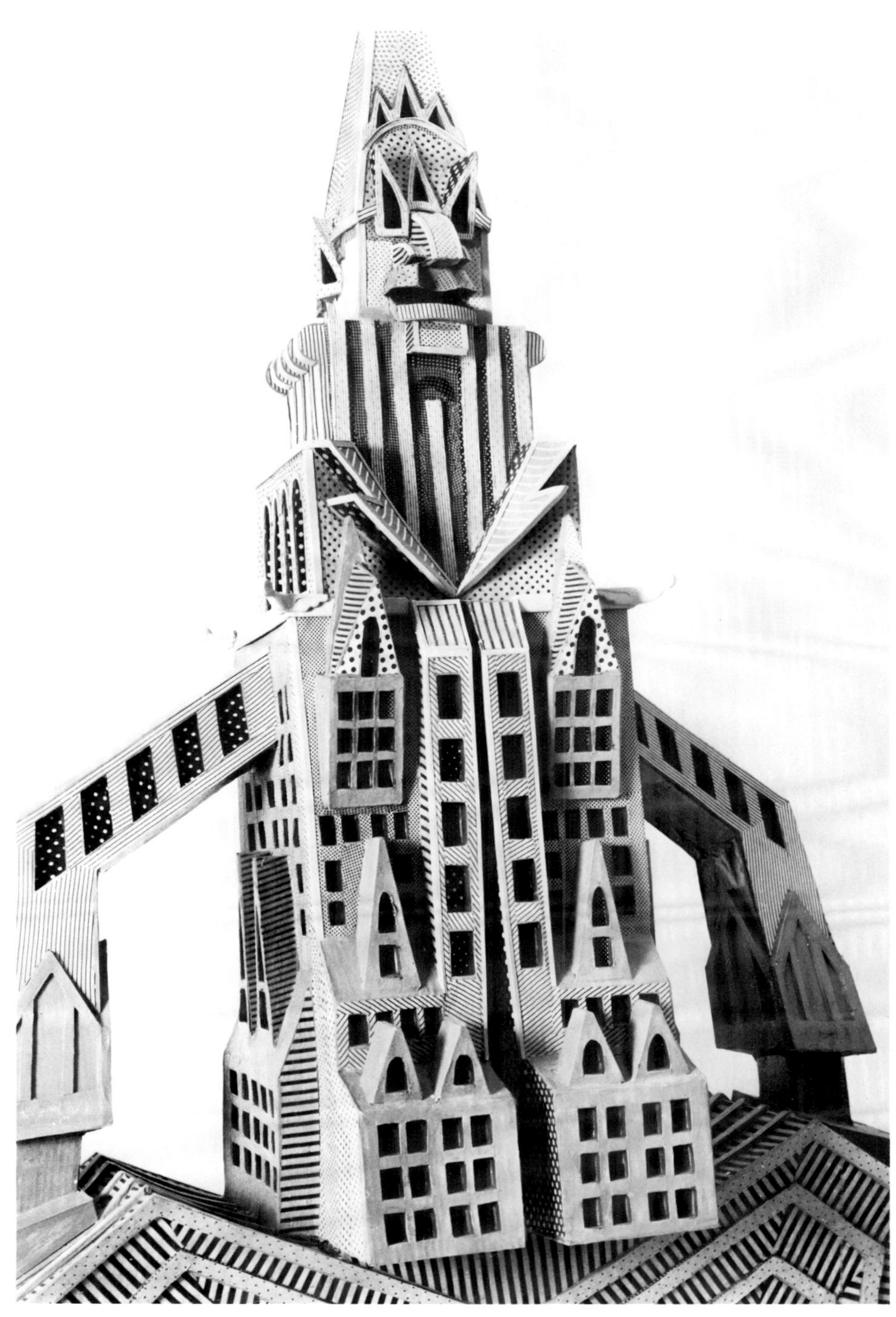

Chrysler Building, 1984	*Kneeling Building,* 1984	*City Hall Building,* 1984	*Soho Building,* 1984
wood, cardboard, cloth, and paint	wood, cardboard, cloth, and paint	wood, cardboard, cloth, and paint	wood, cardboard, cloth, and paint
96 x 42 x 24 inches	84 x 42 x 24 inches	66 x 24 x 36 inches	36 x 30 x 30 inches
Lent by the artist	Lent by the artist	Lent by the artist	Lent by the artist

Russell Hart

Russell Hart's photographs are eerie; they have an air of expectation, as if time has been frozen. Hart's subjects are people and objects seen in the landscape, yet presented so that they often appear isolated and out of context. We see a distilled version of a scene, carefully selected for its formal and psychological implications. Delicately balanced, the relationship of shapes, forms, and tonal ranges in the photographs are keys to their overall compositional integrity.

The three photographs in this exhibition represent Hart's experimentations with the bromoil process, a technique developed at the turn of the century. It is a painterly method whereby ink is brushed or rolled onto a bleached print, allowing for the artist's touch to be more direct and selective. The effect is very graphic, so much that Hart's photographs could be mistaken for pencil or charcoal drawings. In addition to the bromoil process, Hart uses infrared film, which causes halolike effects around objects and tonal reversals.

The Pictorialist photographers used the bromoil technique (among others) to achieve beautiful, romantic images that often resembled paintings and drawings of the period. Hart's photographs can also evoke other art forms and faraway times and places. The image of people on the beach, for example, recalls Georges Seurat's painting *A Sunday Afternoon on the Island of La Grande Jatte* (1884-61). Yet the photographs are very contemporary in their mood of isolation and mystery.

R.R.L.

Born 1953 in Boston, Massachusetts
Education: School of the Museum of Fine Arts, Boston, Massachusetts; Diploma, 1976; Graduate Certificate, 1977
Tufts University, Medford, Massachusetts; B.F.A., 1976
Dartmouth College, Hanover, New Hampshire; 1971-1973
Residence: Jamaica Plain, Massachusetts, and New York, New York
Current position: Associate Editor, **Popular Photography Magazine**

Selected Individual Exhibitions
1987 Zoë Gallery, Boston, Massachusetts

1986 Washington Square Gallery, Brookline, Massachusetts

1984, 1983 Pennington Galleries, Nashville, Tennessee

Selected Group Exhibitions
1987 Museum of Fine Arts, Boston, Massachusetts, *The Nineteenth Traveling Scholarship Competition*

1985 DeCordova and Dana Museum and Park, Lincoln, Massachusetts, *Unaffiliated: Artists Without Galleries*

1982 Hayden Gallery, Massachusetts Institute of Technology, Cambridge, Massachusetts, *Local Visions II: The Beach*

1981 Carpenter Center for Visual Arts, Harvard University, Cambridge, Massachusetts, *Second Sight*

1980 Addison Gallery of American Art, Phillips Academy, Andover, Massachusetts

Selected Bibliography
1986 Kelly Wise. "Litwack's Time Capsule; Hart's Transfer Prints." *Boston Globe*, April 19, 1986, p. 13.

Maryellen Sullivan. "Russell Hart: Photographs." *Views: The Journal of Photography in New England*, Fall 1986, pp. 14-15.

1982 Christine Temin. "Ramon de Los Reyes Spanish Dance Theatre." *Boston Globe*, September 1982.

1980 Michael Pretzer. *Views: The Journal of Photography in New England*, June 1980.

Selected Fellowships and Awards
1987 Alumni Traveling Fellowship, Boston Museum of Fine Arts, Boston, Massachusetts

1981 Clarissa Bartlett Traveling Fellowship, Boston Museum of Fine Arts, Boston, Massachusetts

1977 Albert H. Whitin Traveling Fellowship, Boston Museum of Fine Arts, Boston, Massachusetts

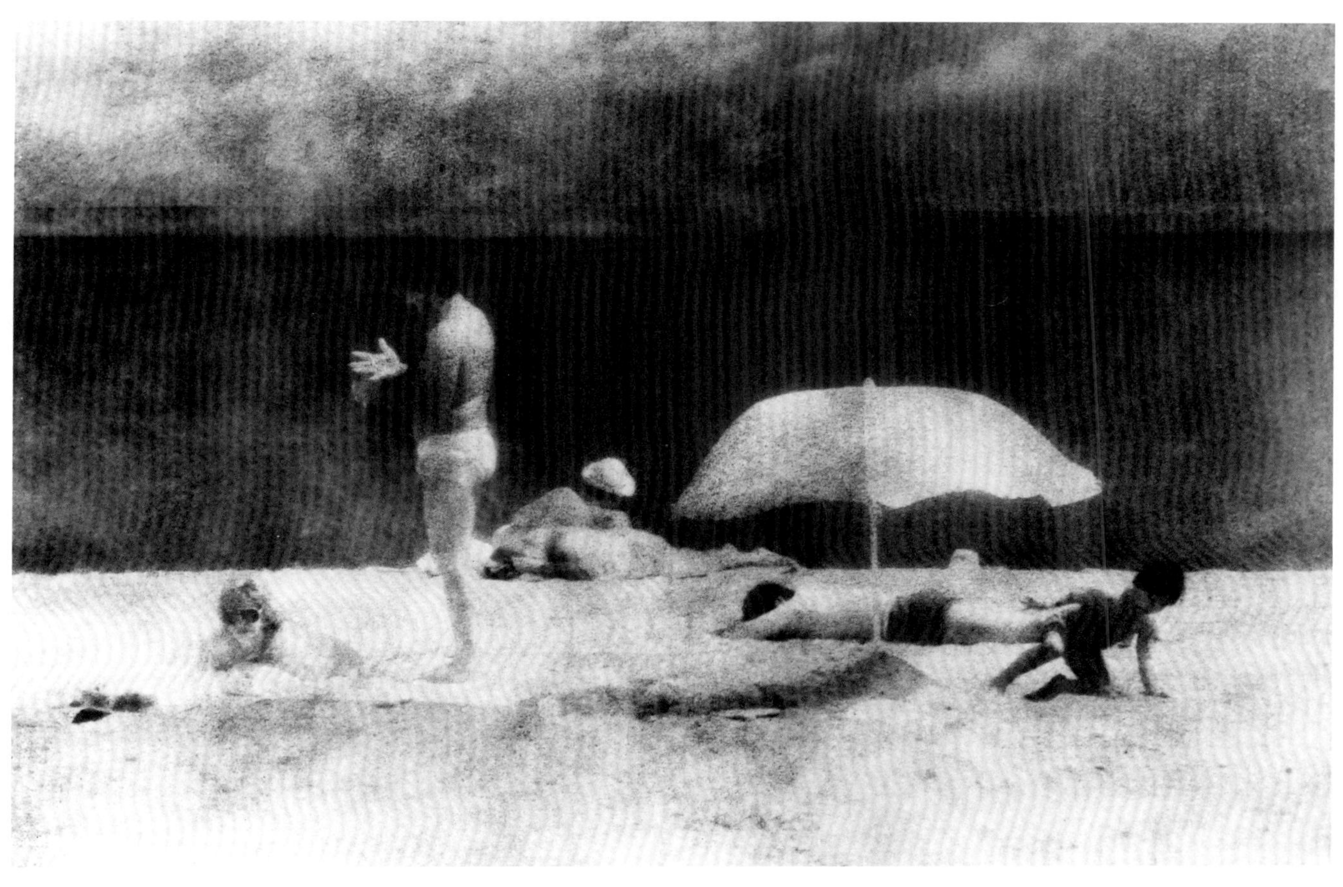

* Untitled, 1987
bromoil print
7¼ x 10⅞ inches
Lent by the artist

Untitled, 1987
bromoil print
7½ x 10⅞ inches
Lent by the artist

Untitled, 1987
bromoil print
7⅜ x 10⅞ inches
Lent by the artist

Marcy Hermansader

Although trained in sculpture and film, Marcy Hermansader has chosen to pursue drawing as her primary means of expression. She grew up in Connecticut of Pennsylvania Dutch parents who had left their traditional community to become artists. After graduation she traveled in China and Mexico. Since 1980 she has lived in Putney, Vermont, where she has occasionally taught drawing at local colleges and at the University of Vermont.

Hermansader's drawings in this exhibition represent a significant departure from her previous work. The subtle uses of color in her new work appear monochromatic. She continues to work on paper; in this series she has selected a white or light ground rather than the black or colored ground she has usually used before. She has consistently used colored pencil accented with acrylic paint, crayon, gold leaf, and watercolor, using thread, netting, fabric, glitter, and paper as collage elements. The processes of cutting, tearing, scratching the surface, and gluing layers of paper underneath the drawings while making small flaps to expose these, transform the paper's surface to create a semblance of other materials. Her drawing becomes a rich, complex patterning.

Hermansader's work is visionary and dreamlike, even somewhat surreal in its search for the interconnectedness of the personal with the external world. Her drawings frequently have direct literary sources, are expressions of her dreams, or reflect her social and political consciousness. Hermansader's work today has a depth, a spiritual quality, and a subtlety of expression that marks a growing maturation in the strength of the emotive qualities.

I.H.

Born 1951 in Glen Cove, New York
Education: Philadelphia College of Art,
Philadelphia, Pennsylvania; B.F.A., 1973
Residence: Putney, Vermont

Selected Individual Exhibitions
1986, 1983 Janet Fleisher Gallery, Philadelphia, Pennsylvania

1983 The Pennsylvania Academy of the Fine Arts, Philadelphia, Pennsylvania

1982 Brattleboro Museum & Art Center, Brattleboro, Vermont

1981, 1980 Eric Makler Gallery, Philadelphia, Pennsylvania

1978 Bethel Gallery, Bethel, Connecticut

Selected Group Exhibitions
1987 Calvin-Morris Gallery, New York, New York, *Neo-Alchemy*

1986 The Clocktower, New York, New York, *Letters*

1985 University Gallery of Fine Art, Ohio State University, Columbus, Ohio, *Rape*

Robert Hull Fleming Museum, University of Vermont, Burlington, Vermont, *Poet-Artist Collaboration*

1984 University Gallery, University of Massachusetts at Amherst, Amherst, Massachusetts, *Domestic Tales*

DeCordova and Dana Museum and Park, Lincoln, Massachusetts, *Contemporary New England Still Life* (traveling exhibition)

1981 Robert Hull Fleming Museum, *A Class Reunion*

Selected Bibliography
1986 Ann Jarmusch. "Marcy Hermansader Janet Fleisher." *Artnews* 85 (Summer 1986), p. 132.

1985 William Zimmer. "Enigmatic Interiors at Noyes." *New York Times,* August 25, 1985, Section 11, p. 20.

1983 Ann-Sargent Wooster. "Marcy Hermansader at the Pennsylvania Academy of Fine Arts." *Art in America* 72 (May 1984), p. 183.

Selected Fellowships and Awards
1985 Residency Fellowship, Blue Mountain Center, Adirondacks, New York

1982 Residency Fellowship, Genesis Program, Ossabaw Island, Georgia

Artist Grant, Vermont Council on the Arts

1977 Fellowship, National Endowment for the Arts

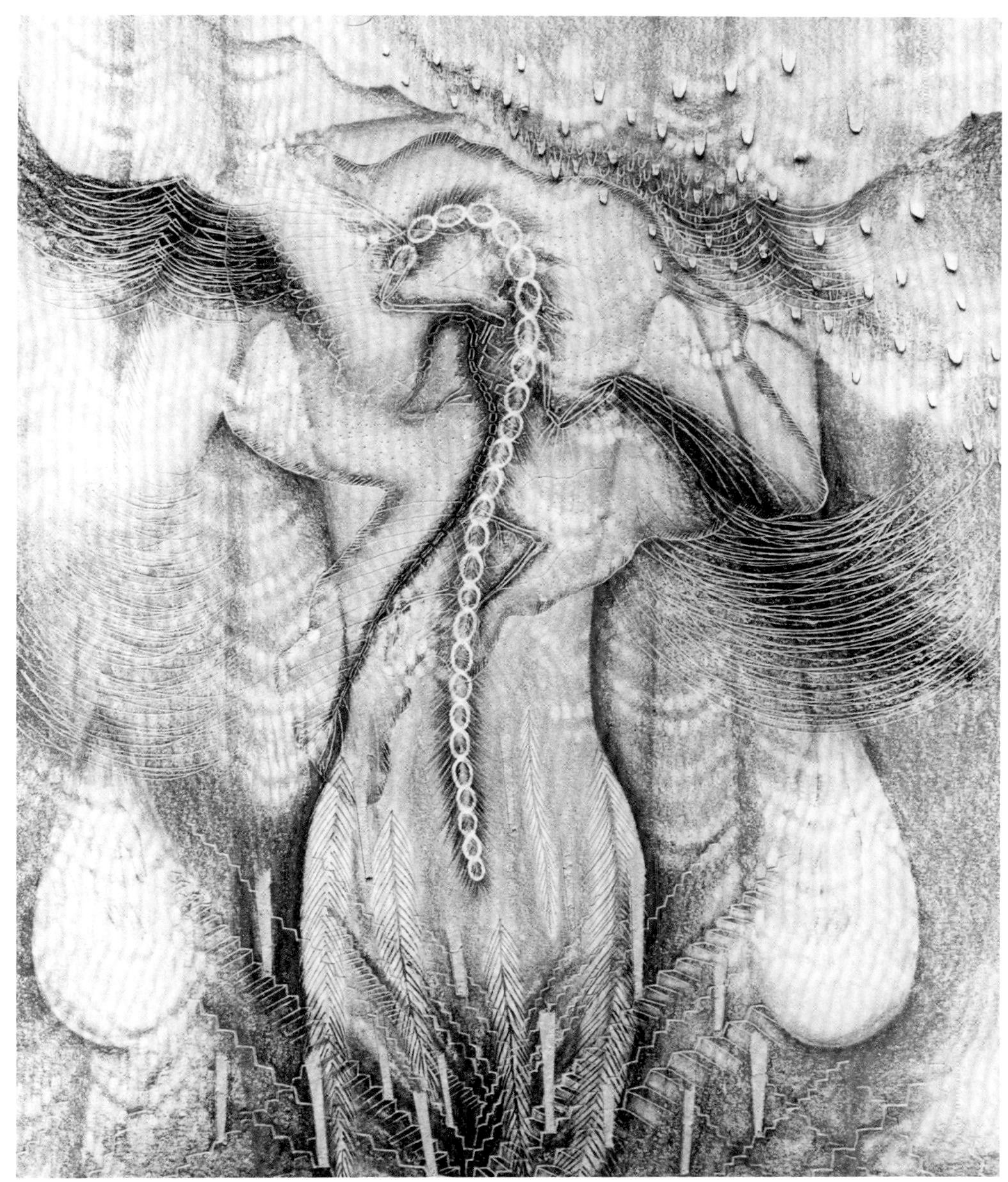

* *The Evolution of Flightlessness,* 1986
mixed media on museum board
17¾ x 14⅝ inches
Lent by the artist

Transparent Being Series, 1986
Untitled (1-86)
mixed media on museum board
18 x 14½ inches
Lent by the artist

Transparent Being Series, 1986
Untitled (2-86)
mixed media on museum board
19 x 14 inches
Lent by the artist

Transparent Being Series, 1986
Untitled (4-86)
mixed media on paper
18 x 15 inches
Lent by the artist

Transparent Being Series, 1986
Untitled (6-86)
mixed media on museum board
20 x 16¼ inches
Lent by the artist

Transparent Being Series, 1986
Untitled (5-86)
mixed media on museum board
20 x 14 inches
Lent by the artist

Christopher Hewat

Christopher Hewat is a sculptor who lives in Connecticut and works in wood. During the past few years, he has produced a series of rectangular screens and fans, relief sculptures with inlaid wood elements. His work exhibits a sensitivity to color and texture which is complemented by his patient craftsmanship.

The screen form has many associations, especially Oriental ones. These precedents, coupled with the modular order of the screen and a suggestive sense of visual movement created by Hewat's inlaid forms, suggest a recounting of events. His vision is unique in contemporary sculpture.

Christopher Hewat said of his work: "I know very little about where my work comes from. The clearest and most compelling of my images appear to me as dreams.

"One night several years ago, I dreamed I was in outer space, twirling weightlessly. The sky seemed endless, and all around me in the darkness there blew a kind of space-debris, miscellaneous polygons, and scraps of unusual color.

"When I woke I wrote down the dream—it seemed remarkable to me—and thought no more about it.

"And then, without my recognizing it for what it was, this small, odd nocturnal image appropriated my hands, and eyes, and all my attention. It seemed to have an inexhaustible power, and fueled nearly two years of feverish work.

"After this I realized that I might accomplish as much by sleeping as by working in the studio."

D.C.D.

Born 1949 in New York, New York
Education: Sarah Lawrence College,
Bronxville, New York; B.A., 1972
Residence: Salisbury, Connecticut

Selected Individual Exhibitions
1984 Victoria Munroe Gallery, New York, New York

1980 Washington Square East Gallery, New York, New York, *Selected Works from the Collection of the Musée Ruse*

Selected Group Exhibitions
1985 Light Gallery, New York, New York, *Messages From 1985*

Victoria Munroe Gallery, *Recent Painting and Sculpture*

1984 Court Gallery, for the benefit of the C.G. Jung Foundation, New York, New York, *Image Pilgrimage*

1983 Impressions Gallery, New York, New York, *New Year Salon Exhibition*

Gabriele Beyers Gallery, New York, New York, *Extra Critical Role*

1982 White Columns, New York, New York, *Shoe Boxes*

1980 New York University, New York, New York, Artists in Residence, Museum Program

Selected Bibiography
1980 Dale McConathy. "Christopher Hewat's Artful Museum." *Arts Canada,* December 1980/January 1981, pp. 21-23.

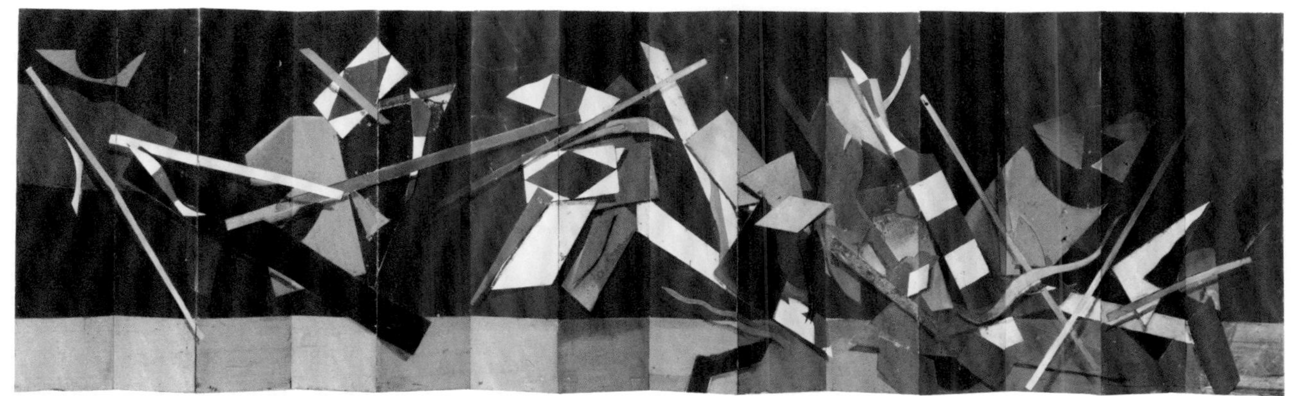

* *Musée Ruse #748,*
"She Loves Me/Loves Me Not," 1985
painted and inlaid wood constuction
29 x 92½ x 4⅜ inches
Courtesy of Victoria Munroe Gallery

Jonathan Imber

For ten years before Jonathan Imber began to paint allegorical figures and portraits, he painted the landscape. After a long period in Boston, during which he developed a distinctive figurative style—expressionistic and psychological—Imber returned to the landscape in 1985.

Although the landscape is only used as background, it reappears for the first time in the 1985 painting *Captive,* in which two typically large figures who almost fill the canvas are placed against an open sky and grassy field. In the landscapes that followed, such as *Bog,* figures are totally absent, and the emphasis is on capturing the essence of a place, with its attendant conditions of light, weather, and mood.

Always one to acknowledge his sources of inspiration, Imber cites among his mentors Philip Guston, who was his teacher, Max Beckmann, Rembrandt, and Paul Cézanne. Yet the most obvious source for *Bog* is the work of Vincent Van Gogh, and even the marshlands in the picture (actually a farm in upstate New York) recall the lowlands of Van Gogh's native Holland.

Imber's figurative paintings and landscapes, although seemingly quite different, have much in common. The thick, pronounced Imber brushstroke, which causes body tones in the figure paintings to vibrate, enables blades of grass to stand out individually in the landscapes. The sense of anticipation and unexplained mystery is more pronounced in the allegorical figure paintings, yet the landscapes also resonate with a psychological depth which elevates them above the plane of pure representation.

R.R.L.

Born 1950 in New York, New York
Education: Boston University, Boston,
Massachusetts; M.F.A., 1977
Cornell University, Ithaca, New York;
B.F.A., 1972
Residence: Somerville, Massachusetts

Selected Individual Exhibitions
1987, 1985 Victoria Munroe Gallery, New York, New York

1986, 1982, 1981 Nielsen Gallery, Boston, Massachusetts

Selected Group Exhibitions
1986 Portland Museum of Art, Portland, Maine, *The Vinalhaven Press*

Jewish Museum, New York, New York, *Jewish Themes/Contemporary American Artists II*

DeCordova and Dana Museum and Park, Lincoln, Massachusetts, *Expressionism in Boston: 1945-1985*

Rose Art Museum, Brandeis University, Waltham, Massachusetts, *Twenty-fifth Anniversary Exhibition*

1985 Albright-Knox Art Gallery, Buffalo, New York, *Awards in the Visual Arts 4* (traveling exhibition)

1983 Institute of Contemporary Art, Boston, Massachusetts, *Boston Now*

1980 Fogg Art Museum, Harvard University, Cambridge, Massachusetts, *Made in Boston: Contemporary Drawings from the Permanent Collection*

Selected Bibliography
1987 Anita Daimant. "Face to Face." *Boston Magazine* 79 (May 1987), p. 160.

1986 Nancy Stapen. "Jon Imber." *Artforum* 25 (September 1986), pp. 137-138.

Michael Brenson. "Bringing Fresh Approaches to Age Old Jewish Themes." *New York Times,* August 3, 1986, p. H27.

1985 William Corbett. "Jon Imber." *Arts Magazine* 59 (April 1985), p. 11

1982 Christopher Swan. "Portrait of the Artist." *Christian Science Monitor,* October 28, 1982.

Pam Allara. "Issues: New Allegory." *Artnews* 81 (May 1982), pp. 146-149.

1981 Lois Tarlow. "Jon Imber: Painter." *Art New England* 2 (November 1981), p. 14.

Selected Fellowships and Awards
1986 Massachusetts Arts Lottery Award, Massachusetts Arts Lottery Council, Boston, Massachusetts

1985 Massachusetts Artists Fellowship, Artists Foundation, Boston, Massachusetts

The Engelhard Award, Engelhard Foundation, Cambridge, Massachusetts

1984 Award in the Visual Arts, Southeastern Center for Contemporary Art, Winston-Salem, North Carolina

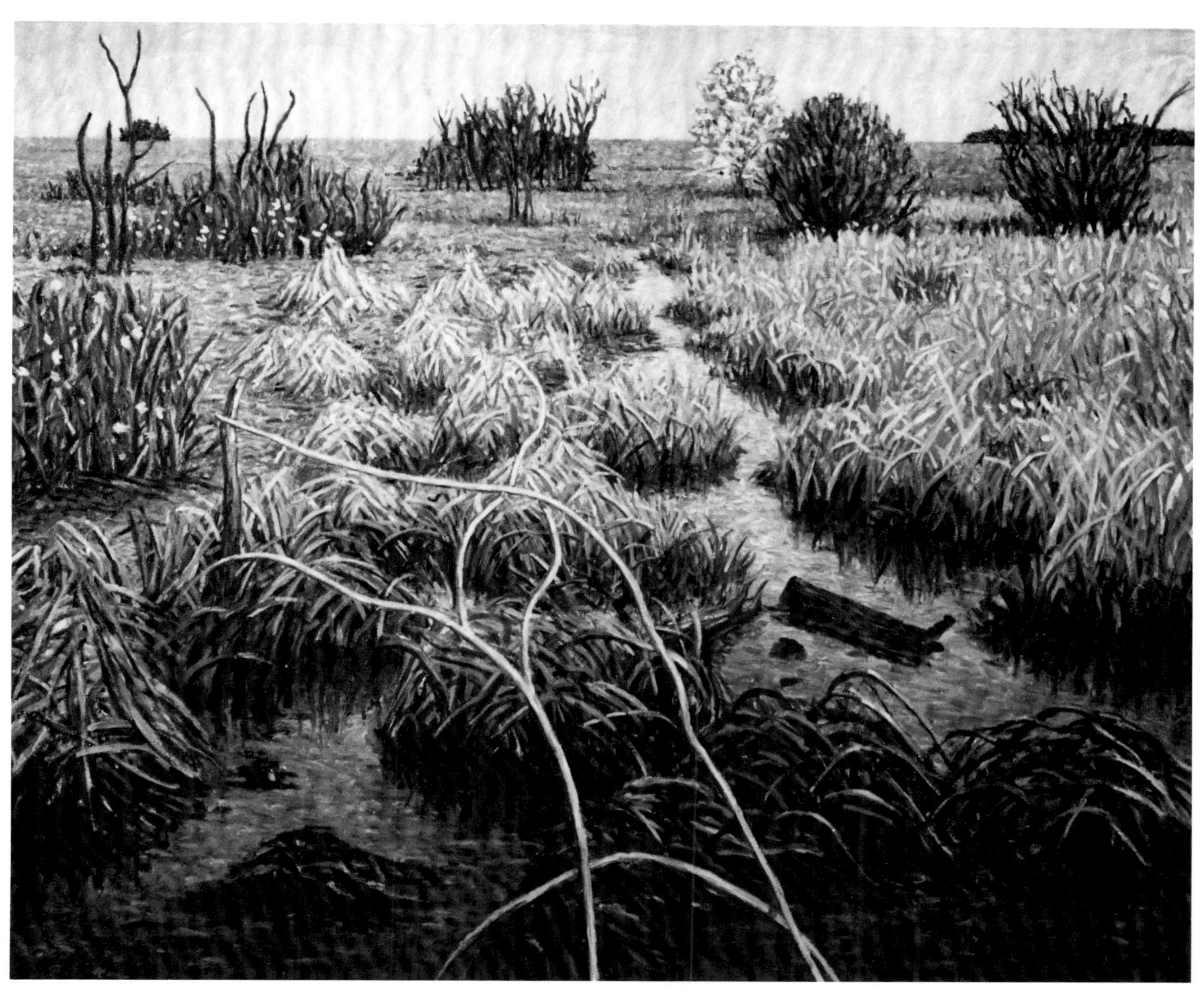

* *Bog,* 1986-87
oil on canvas
66 x 80 inches
Courtesy of Victoria Munroe Gallery
New York, New York

Maureen McCabe

Maureen McCabe has produced collages for more than two decades. Her assemblages are the products of associations she makes between the materials used and an implied narrative or purely visual idea. McCabe surrounds herself in the studio with the materials of her art: hundreds of different kinds of papers, feathers, prints, furs, and objects she has collected over the years. She finds them at flea markets, yard sales, antique shops, and print dealers' shops, and sometimes gets them from friends.

The sea shells in the work *Gray/Brown Lizard,* for instance, were collected by her friend Muriel Castle. "She used to walk on the beach with her father and pick up these shells (he was old and dying and this was something they could still do together). She always liked my work. Muriel's c. 70 herself. She wanted me to have the collection of the walks. To me this *(Gray/Brown Lizard)* is one of my most successful pieces in terms of almost perfect camouflage. I wish I could repeat it sometimes, but this kind of timing is rare. Also, it's the only piece I've done this quickly! Everything worked and fell together. What a joy!"

Sometimes, as in *Art Deco Zebras,* the materials may have waited many years to be used. In this particular work the art deco paper had been collected by the artist in 1965 and used in the work in 1985. In other works, such as *Fate* (1986), the idea for the work had been evolving for years.

D.C.D.

Born 1947 in Quincy, Massachusetts
Education: Cranbrook Academy of Art,
Bloomfield Hills, Michigan; M.F.A., 1971
Rhode Island School of Design,
Providence, Rhode Island; B.F.A., 1969
Residence: Quaker Hill, Connecticut
Current position: Professor of Studio Art,
Connecticut College, New London,
Connecticut

Selected Individual Exhibitions

1987 Gallery K., Washington, D.C. Periodic exhibitions since 1972.

1985 Barry Friedman, Ltd., New York, New York

1983 Marianne Deson Gallery, Chicago, Illinois

1981 Lyman Allyn Museum, New London, Connecticut

1979 Carlson Gallery, University of Bridgeport, Connecticut

1978 Phyllis Kind Gallery, Chicago, Illinois

1977, 1975, 1972 Allan Stone Gallery, New York, New York

Selected Group Exhibitions

1985 Museo Tamayo, Mexico City, Mexico *Imagenes en Cajas*

1983 Washington Project for the Arts, Washington, D.C., *Poetic Objects*

1982-83 Neuberger Museum, State University of New York, Purchase, New York, *Area Code 914-203*

1981 Renwick Gallery of the National Museum of American Art, Smithsonian Institution, Washington, D.C., *Animal Images*

1978 Cité Internationale des Arts, Paris, France

Connecticut College, New London, Connecticut; *Connecticut Painting, Drawing, and Sculpture* (traveling exhibition)

Selected Fellowships and Awards

1980 Individual Artists Grant, Connecticut Commission on the Arts

1976-77 Grant for *Artist and Poet Collaboration,* National Endowment for the Arts

1975 Residency Fellowship, Yaddo Foundation, Saratoga Springs, New York

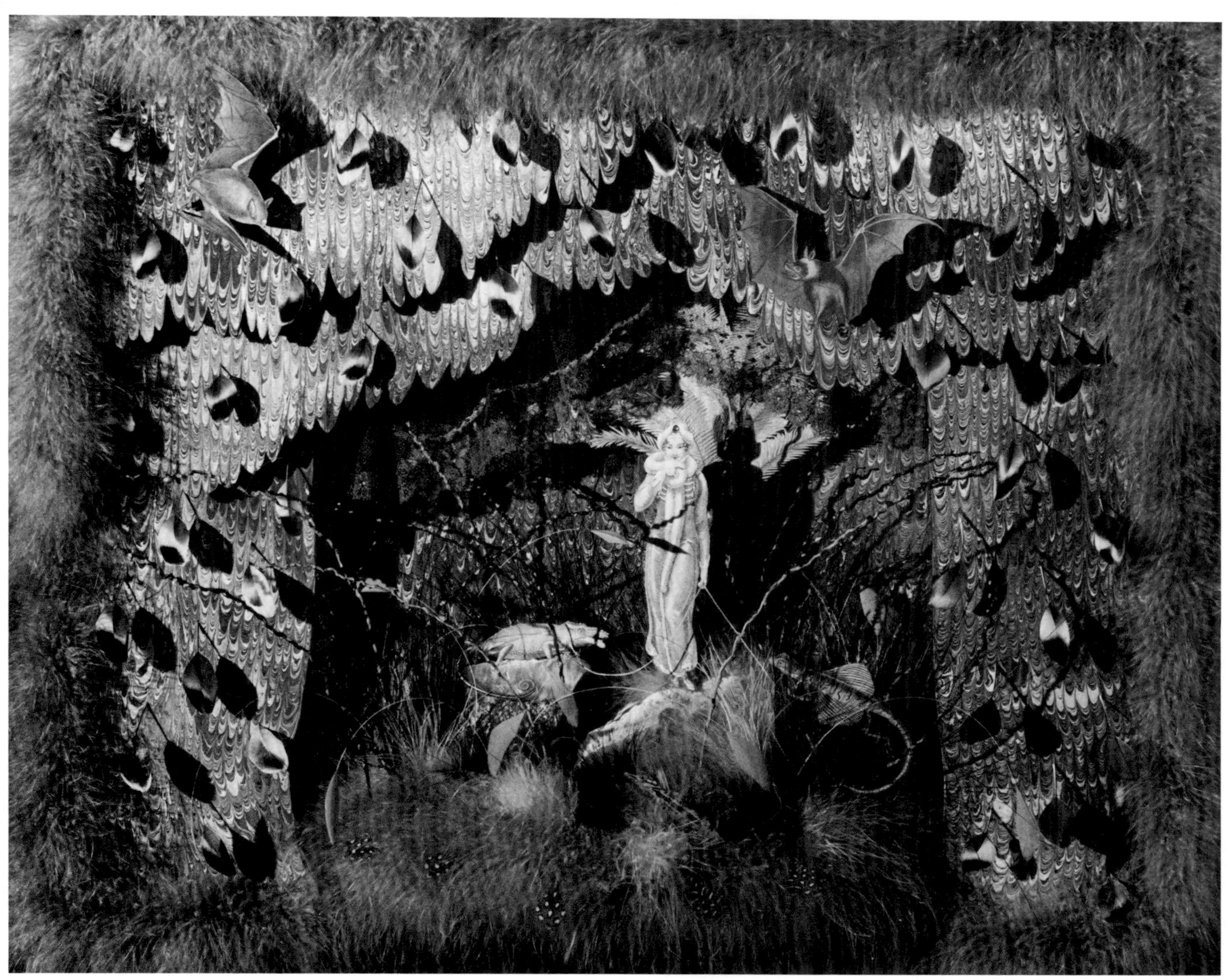

* *Topaz Theater*, 1984
mixed media construction
20 x 24 x 5½ inches
Lent by the artist

Gray/Brown Lizard, 1984
mixed media construction
20 x 16 x 4 inches
Collection of Timothy Egert

Fate, 1986
mixed media construction
20 x 24 x 5½ inches
Lent by the artist

Art Deco Zebras, 1985
mixed media construction
20 x 25 x 4½ inches
Collection of Timothy Egert

Rhino and Dingo, 1984
mixed media construction
20 x 25 x 4½ inches
Collection of Timothy Egert

Mark McDonnell

Mark McDonnell spent his early years in the then-booming city of São Paulo, Brazil, where he became intrigued by building types and methods. He met glass artist Dale Chihuly at Pilchuck and subsequently attended the Rhode Island School of Design, studying architecture as well as glassmaking. At this time McDonnell was attracted by such architects as Richard Morris Hunt and McKim, Mead & White, who exemplified the virtues of formal organization, order, and centrality. His early fascination with fenestration was heightened by a visit to the great greenhouses of mid-nineteenth-century Europe, which are central to his work with glass blocks.

The artist is interested, above all, in light. He thinks of his glass block pieces as participatory works which demand both active and passive involvement of the viewer as they are constantly transformed by changes in the environment.

In recent months McDonnell has attempted to move away from his traditional classical approach to one more romantic and personal. He has begun a series of broken-glass sculptures in which accident and process play a large part and is pursuing, in his sited works, an overtly humanistic approach.

N.R.V.

Born 1954 in Cairo, Egypt
Education: Rhode Island School of Design, Providence, Rhode Island; B.F.A., 1979
Residence: Providence, Rhode Island

Selected Individual Exhibitions

1987, 1986, 1985 Snyderman Gallery, Philadelphia, Pennsylvania

1986, 1985, 1984 Helander Gallery, Palm Beach, Florida

1986 Sarah Squeri Gallery, Cincinnati, Ohio

1985 Newport Art Museum, Newport, Rhode Island, *Labyrinth for a Diva* (installation)

Three Rivers Arts Festival, Pittsburgh, Pennsylvania, *Labyrinth for Three Rivers* (installation)

1985, 1984 Smith Goodrich Gallery, Providence, Rhode Island

1981 Exposição de Vidro, Museu de Arte, São Paulo, Brazil

Selected Group Exhibitions

1987 Herron Gallery, Indianapolis Center for Contemporary Art, Indianapolis, Indiana, *Contemporary Lamps, Tables, and Chairs*

1986 Glasmuseum, Ebeltoft, Denmark

1985 Contemporary Arts Center, Cincinnati, Ohio, *Transparent Motives: Glass on a Large Scale* (traveling exhibition)

Musée des Beaux-Arts, Rouen, France, *Exposition Internationale*

1984 Woods-Gerry Gallery, Rhode Island School of Design, Providence, Rhode Island, *Artists and Disarmament*

Anderson Art Center, Hartwick College, Oneonta, New York, *The New Glass Seen*

1983 Tucson Museum of Art, Tucson, Arizona, *Sculptural Glass*

Selected Bibliography

1986 Carroll West. "Glass: As Sculptural Medium." *International Sculpture* 5 (September/October 1986), p. 8.

1985 Ronald J. Onorato. "Rhode Island: Newport Art Museum/Newport: Mark McDonnell." *Art New England* 6 (October 1985), p. 17.

1983 Christine Robbins. "Sculptural Glass." *American Craft* 43 (August/September 1983), p. 5.

Selected Fellowships and Awards

1987 Individual Artists Fellowship, Rhode Island State Council on the Arts

1983 Artist-in-Residence, Saxe Award, Pilchuck, Stanwood, Washington

1981 Fellowship, National Endowment for the Arts

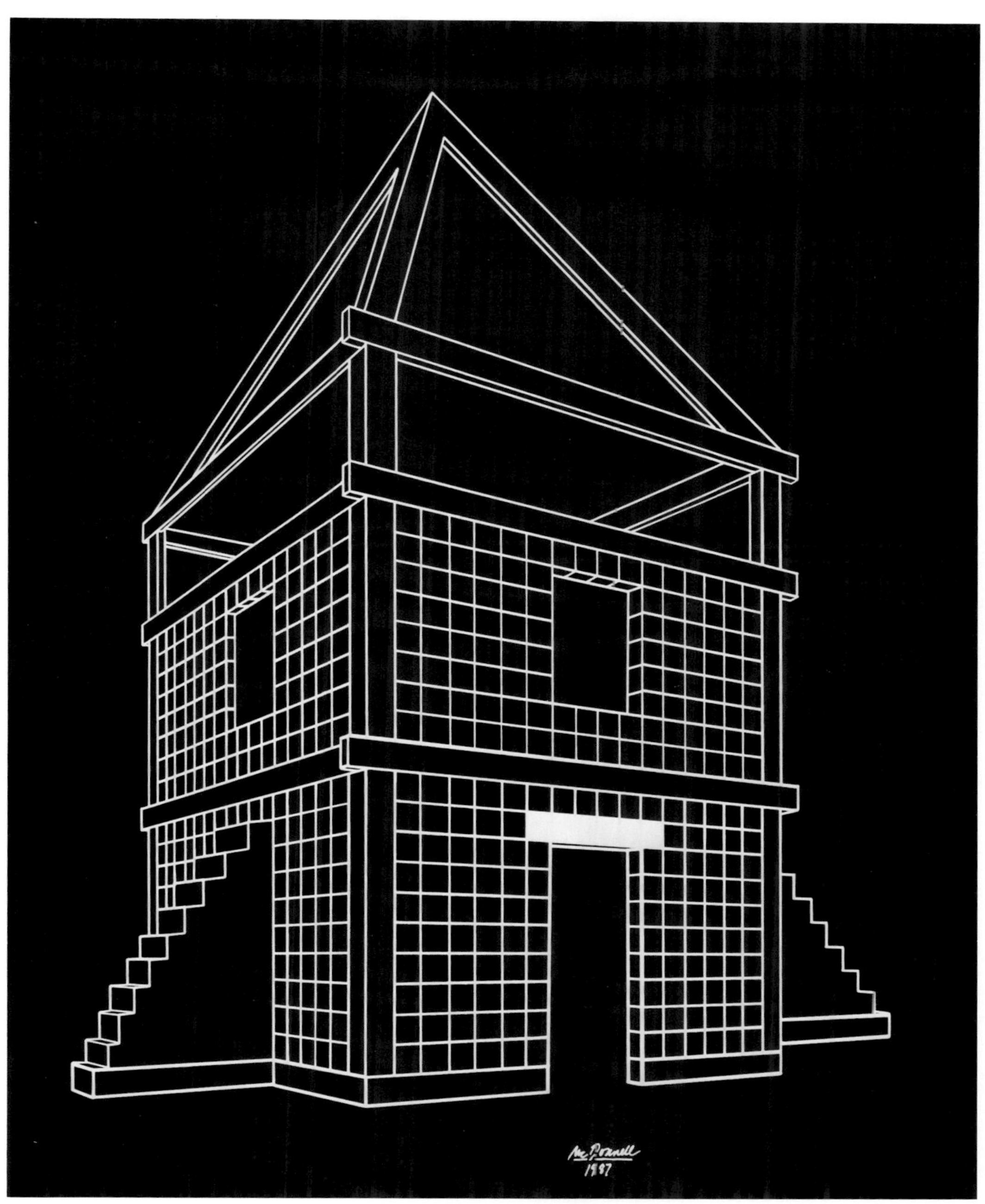

All Along the Watch Tower, 1988
glass block and wood installation
26 x 12 x 24 feet
David Winton Bell Gallery, Brown University,
Providence, Rhode Island
Glass blocks donated by
Pittsburgh Corning Corporation

* *Study for "All Along the Watch Tower,"* 1987
photostat
28 x 22 inches
Lent by the artist

John McNamara

John McNamara's paintings have long been identified with abstraction, yet elements of figuration and representation appear often. Much of his work refers to the landscape by either explicitly or abstractly depicting trees, mountains, and water. The new paintings shown in this exhibition are more abstract and less specific in the associations they invoke. They are landscapes of the mind.

In the past McNamara has worked primarily on canvas, often on an epic scale, with some paintings measuring up to twenty-one feet in width. The balance of abstraction versus representation has varied in each new McNamara series, as has the thickness and color of the paint. The latest paintings, the largest of which are four by five feet, are done on birch plywood and present a more immediate and fluid impression. Painted wet on wet, they have a high gloss surface which emphasizes the thin and liquid process by which they were painted. There has also been a shift from dark to light color and from thick to thin paint.

In their spontaneity and ability to conjure up a multitude of associations on a subconscious level, the paintings recall the automatic paintings produced by the surrealists in the 1920s and 1930s. The loose network of lines for which McNamara is well known is still present, particularly in *Abstract Painting #6,* where the shape circumscribed by the curved line suggests the trajectory of a roller coaster. The mood conveyed in these paintings is cheerful, the color vibrant, the surfaces appealing.

R.R.L.

Born 1950 in Cambridge, Massachusetts
Education: Massachusetts College of Art,
Boston, Massachusetts; B.F.A., 1971;
M.F.A., 1977
Residence: Brookline, Massachusetts
Current position: Associate Professor of
Art, Massachusetts College of Art,
Boston, Massachusetts

Selected Individual Exhibitions
1987, 1985 Stavaridis Gallery, Boston, Massachusetts

1987 Honolulu Academy of Fine Arts, Honolulu, Hawaii

1986 Massachusetts College of Art, Boston, Massachusetts

1986, 1985, 1984 Bess Cutler Gallery, New York, New York

1982 The Exhibition Space at 112 Green Street, New York, New York

Selected Group Exhibitions
1987 The Brockton Art Museum/Fuller Memorial, Brockton, Massachusetts, *Fifth Brockton Triennial*

1986 Museum of Fine Arts, Boston, Massachusetts, *Boston Collects*

DeCordova and Dana Museum and Park, Lincoln, Massachusetts, *Expressionism in Boston: 1945-1985*

1983 Southeastern Center for Contemporary Art, Winston-Salem, North Carolina, *Awards in the Visual Arts 2* (traveling exhibition)

1982 The Currier Gallery of Art, Manchester, New Hampshire, *New England Painters*

1981 Institute of Contemporary Art, Boston, Massachusetts, *Boston Now: Abstract Painting*

1978 Rose Art Museum, Brandeis University, Waltham, Massachusetts, *Fresh Images*

Selected Bibliography
1986 Maurice Poirer. "John McNamara." *Artnews* 85 (September 1986), pp. 130-131.

Theodore Wolff. "Young Talent on the Trail of Greatness." *Christian Science Monitor,* April 14, 1986.

1984 Gerrit Henry. "John McNamara at Bess Cutler." *Art in America* 72 (Summer 1984), p. 166.

1983 Theodore Wolff. "The Many Masks of Modern Art." *Christian Science Monitor,* April 7, 1983, p. 20.

1982 Carl Belz. "John McNamara." *Arts Magazine* 57 (November 1982), p. 13.

Kenneth Baker. "Abstracting Reality." *Boston Phoenix,* March 23, 1982, p. 10.

1980 Elizabeth Findley. "John McNamara at Cutler/Stavaridis." *Art in America* 68 (September 1980), p. 130.

Selected Fellowships and Awards
1986, 1983, 1980 Massachusetts Artists Fellowship, Artists Foundation, Boston, Massachusetts

1982 Award in the Visual Arts, Southeastern Center for Contemporary Art, Winston-Salem, North Carolina

1981 Fellowship, National Endowment for the Arts

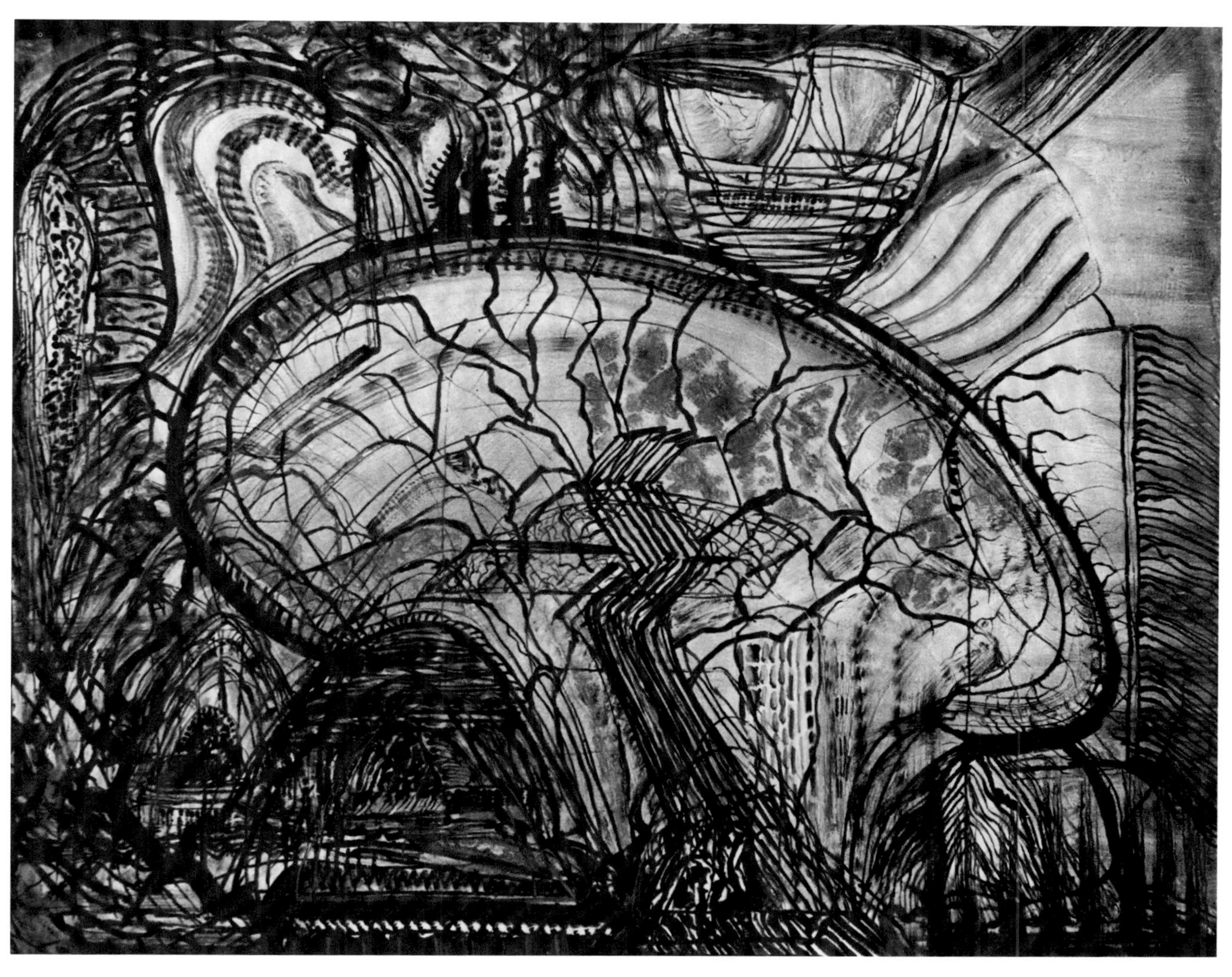

<table>
<tr><td>* Abstract Painting #6, 1987
oil on birch plywood
48 x 60 inches
Lent by the artist</td><td>Abstract Painting #4, 1987
oil on birch plywood
48 x 60 inches
Lent by the artist</td></tr>
</table>

Denny Moers

Denny Moers has been consumed by an interest in photography since he was twelve. He met Aaron Siskind at the Visual Studies Workshop, visited him in Rhode Island, and subsequently moved to Rhode Island to join what he perceived as an intellectually intact community of artists. Proximity to New York has always been important to Moers. His primary source of inspiration is contemporary art, especially those works which emphasize texture and light.

Moers consistently centers his attention on the individual print and does not exploit photography's potential as a duplicating medium. He regards the photographic paper as a blank canvas, a sensitized arena capable of absorbing and reflecting light, from which he derives a latent image.

The image, however, is never the dominant factor. The literal world is not simply recorded, but is transformed. In his early Providence years arcane architectural details provided source material for highly abstracted works. More recently, travels to Turkey, Yugoslavia, and Egypt have triggered a complex set of responses from which the artist creates a sense of the presence and meaning of ancient sites in the twentieth century. The pervasive power of this imagery has become somewhat disturbing to Moers, who now senses in his work a transition to greater abstraction.

N.R.V.

Born 1953 in Detroit, Michigan
Education: Visual Studies Workshop,
Rochester, New York
Residence: Lincoln, Rhode Island

Selected Individual Exhibitions
1987 Museum of Art, Rhode Island School of Design, Providence, Rhode Island

1986 Carlo Lamagna Gallery, New York, New York

1985, 1980 Thomas Segal Gallery, Boston, Massachusetts

1985, 1983, 1981 O.K. Harris Gallery, New York, New York

1984 Center for Creative Photography, University of Arizona, Tucson, Arizona

Paule Pia Gallery, Antwerp, Belgium

1982 Manuel Alvarez Bravo Gallery, Mexico City, Mexico

Selected Group Exhibitions
1987 Palazzo Avela, Turin, Italy, *Torino Photographia Biennale*

Addison Gallery of American Art, Andover, Massachusetts, *Invitational*

School 33 Art Center, Baltimore, Maryland, *Architecture as a State of Mind*

1986 Galerie Photographique de la Bibliothèque Nationale, Paris, France, *Récents enrichissements ou dix photographes pour demain*

1984 Galleria d'Arte del Cavallino, Venice, Italy, *Invitational*

David Winton Bell Gallery, Brown University, Providence, Rhode Island, *Some Photographic Uses of Color*

1983 International Museum of Photography at George Eastman House, Rochester, New York, *Miller/Plummer Collection of Photography*

Selected Bibliography
1987 Vicki Goldberg. "Photographing the Good Stuff: How the Camera Looks at Other Kinds of Art." *American Photographer* 18 (January 1987), p. 24.

1986 E.L. Klein, "Exhibition at Carlo Lamagna Gallery." *Arts Magazine* 61 (December 1986), p. 120.

1984 Marsha Miro. "A Golden Age for Non-Traditional Art." *Detroit Free Press,* September 23, 1984.

1983 Joan Murray. "Poetic Beauty." *Artweek* 14 (October 8, 1983), p. 16.

Gene Thornton. "In the Arts: Critics Choices: Photography." *New York Times,* May 15, 1983, section 2A, p. 3.

1981 Steve Pollack. "Brushes with Light." *Camera Arts* 1, November/December 1981.

Selected Fellowships and Awards
1984, 1979 Individual Artist's Fellowship, Rhode Island State Council on the Arts

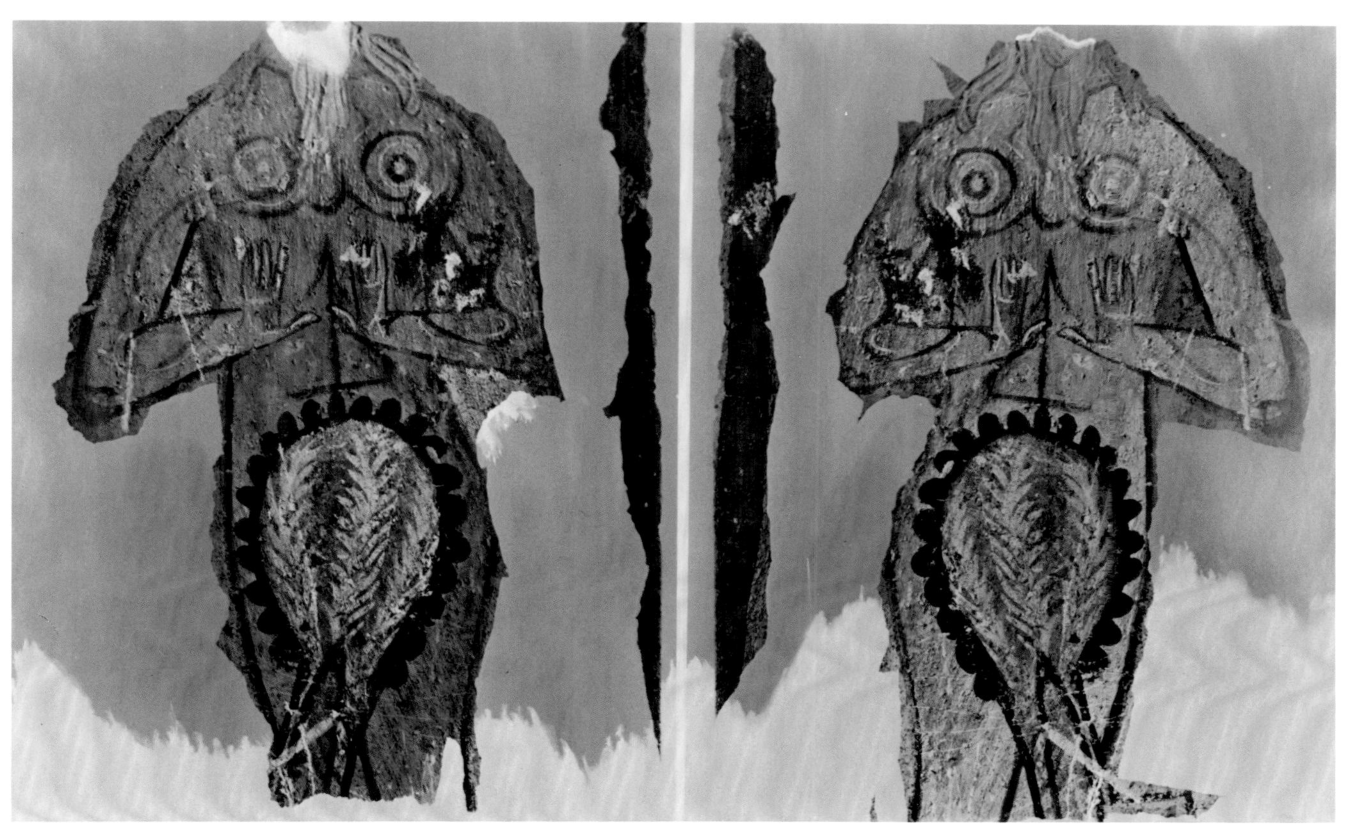

Digressions of an Angel #3:
In Cappadocia, 1985
photographic monoprint
16 x 20 inches
Lent by the artist

* An Ancient Struggle #3, 1985-86
photographic monoprints (diptych)
each print: 16 x 20 inches
Lent by the artist

The Kiss, 1986
photographic monoprint
16 x 20 inches
Lent by the artist

Marjorie Moore

Not long ago we would have typed Marjorie Moore as an astute and social satirist. She had—and still has—an eye for the offbeat and the truly preposterous. Yet her humor served mainly to sugar a moral critique of our life on the vinyl frontier.

In her recent work—since 1983—Moore has widened and deepened her critique. She now protests our self-willed and ultimately self-destructive separation from nature and from our natural selves. She protests our efforts to conquer, tame, break, master, and trivialize the earth. For Moore, nature is not the polite lady with the parasol who nannies babes in the woods. Nature is whatever prowls free beyond the picket fence or flees the advance of the bulldozer.

The volatility of these ideas has forced radical changes upon her visual language and delivery. No longer reliant upon commentary, she favors a darker, multi-layered reading of the image. Her color too has darkened, expressed by a kinetic drawing style that disintegrates as much as it defines forms. Her imagination has become more dramatic, even melodramatic, inevitably tempting the artist on to the stage. Moore's performance collaborations (*Toying in the Woods* 1986 and *Let's Go See the Animals* 1988) have heightened the theatricality of her painting. Her canvases are often conceived as theater pieces, staged within a shallow space by players from the artist's stock company. In contrast to her earlier work, these are not at all precise in their meanings. But one catches her drift.

J.W.C.

Born 1944 in Akron, Ohio
Education: Syracuse University,
Syracuse, New York; B.F.A, 1966
Residence: Brunswick, Maine

Selected Individual Exhibitions
1986 Andover Gallery, Andover, Massachusetts

1984 The Works Gallery, Philadelphia, Pennsylvania

Helen Bumpus Gallery, Duxbury, Massachusetts

1983, 1980 Barridoff Galleries, Portland, Maine

Cape Split Place, Addison, Maine

Selected Group Exhibitions
1987 Maine Coast Artists Gallery, Rockport, Maine, *Director's Invitational*

1986 The Maine Festival, Brunswick, Maine, *Toying in the Woods* (collaborative performance)

1985 Martina Hamilton Gallery, New York, New York, *Summer Invitational*

Stavaridis Gallery, Boston, Massachusetts, *New Talent*

1984 Bowdoin College Museum of Art, Brunswick, Maine, *Inside/Outside: 1984 Maine Artists Invitational*

Addison Gallery of American Art, Phillips Academy, Andover, Massachusetts, *Sticks*

1983 Boston University Art Gallery, Boston, Massachusetts, *Elements of Landscape*

Selected Bibliography
1987 Susan Elizabeth Ryan. "Five Political Artists in Maine: Marjorie Moore," *Artists in Maine* 2 (Spring 1987), pp. 30-31.

1986 William David Barry, "Marjorie Moore: Toying in the Woods," *Art New England* 8 (December 1986/January 1987), p. 14.

1985 Christine Temin. "Perspectives," *Boston Globe,* August 8, 1985, p. 68.

1984 Edgar Allen Beem. "Inside/Outside Tingles the Eye and the Mind," *Maine Times,* July 6, 1984, p. 25.

John Coffey. "Marjorie Moore: From the Woods," *Art New England* 5 (January 1984), p. 8.

1983 Lois Tarlow. "Alternative Space: Marjorie Moore," *Art New England* 4 (November 1983), pp. 14-15.

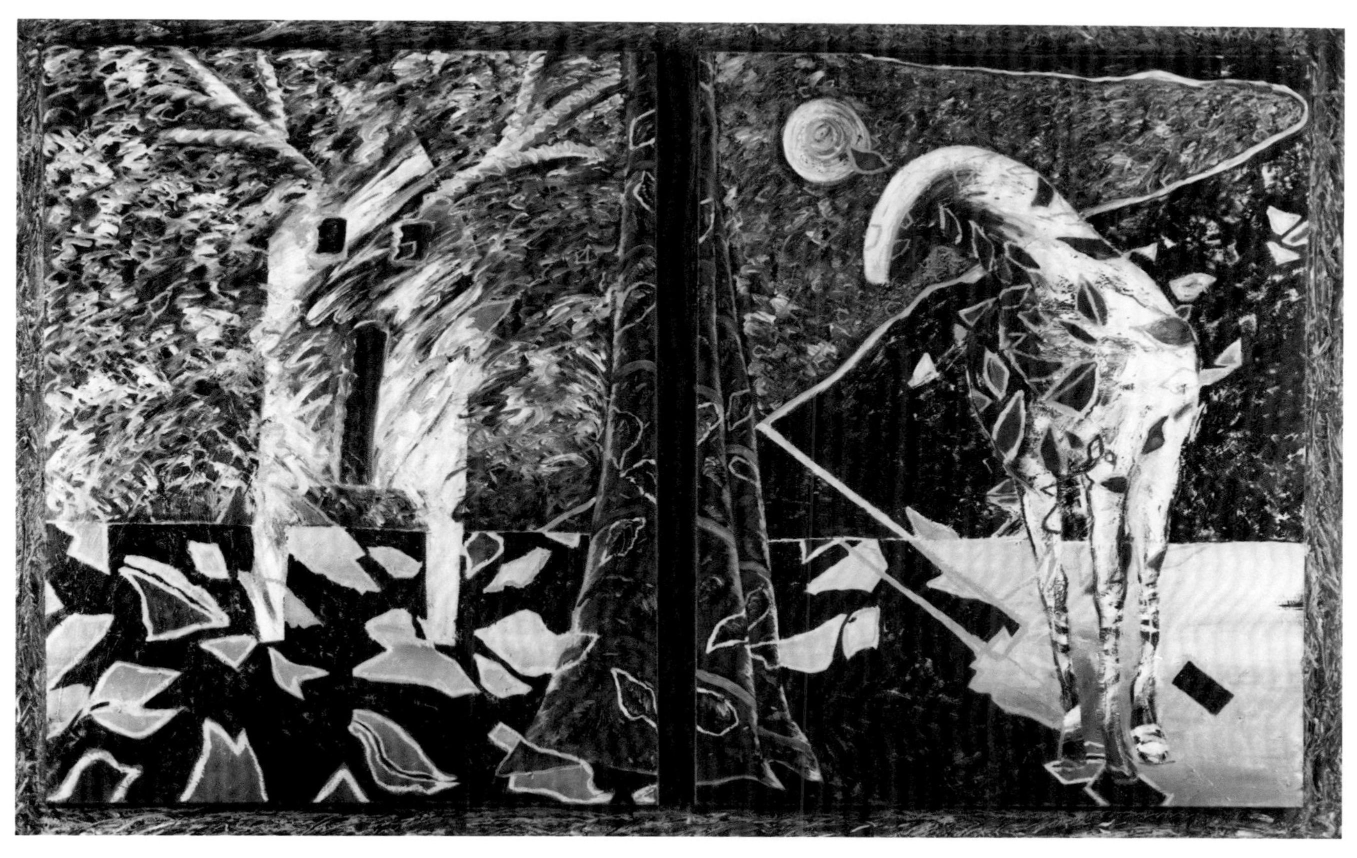

* *Forest Eyes,* 1986
oil on canvas and wood
60 x 91 inches
Courtesy of Howard Yezerski Gallery,
Andover, Massachusetts

Michael Singer

Trained as a painter, Michael Singer turned early in his career to sculpture, gaining international recognition for his large-scale constructions. Raised on Long Island, Singer lived in New York's East Village before moving to Vermont in 1971. With this change in location came a departure from his use of materials and constructs amenable to an urban landscape and his adoption of the use of only organic materials.

Singer's work aims to explore the essence of art and its relationship to the natural world. In the early 1970s he created temporary outdoor structures which he documented with photographs. By the mid-1970s he had adapted his work to interior gallery spaces, his constructions close in feeling to Japanese Shinto shrines. His recent large-scale interior sculptures of wooden beams and slabs of slate, granite, and fieldstone are placed inside a wooden fence or on a platform.

In this exhibition he is represented by a drawing and a print from his 1985 *7 Moon Ritual Series* and an installation piece which will be created and seen only at the Fleming Museum in Vermont. For this print, the result of a collaboration with the printmaker John Hutcheson of New Jersey, Singer cut up photo transparencies of his drawings, using them as "marks," "phrases," and "words" for his own private language. He incorporated images from his previous drawings, using a photographic transfer process. He carefully selected papers to maintain subtle gradations of color, while overlaying transparent papers and cutouts from his drawings. His principally black-and-white drawings of charcoal, chalk, and gouache also incorporate ripped-up pieces of past drawings pasted together and layered tracing paper cutouts.

I.H.

Born 1945 in Brooklyn, New York
Education: Graduate study, Rutgers University, New Brunswick, New Jersey, 1968
Cornell University, Ithaca, New York; B.F.A., 1967
Yale University Norfolk Program, Norfolk, Connecticut, 1966
Residence: Wilmington, Vermont

Selected Individual Exhibitions
1987 State University of New York at Stony Brook, New York

1986, 1981, 1978, 1975 Sperone Westwater, New York, New York

1984 The Solomon R. Guggenheim Museum, New York, New York

1980 Renaissance Society at the University of Chicago, Chicago, Illinois

1979 University Art Museum, Berkeley, California, *Matrix/Berkeley 25: Michael Singer*

1977 Neuberger Museum, State University of New York, Purchase, New York

1976 Wadsworth Atheneum, Hartford, Connecticut, *Matrix 24/Michael Singer*

Selected Group Exhibitions
1985 The Solomon R. Guggenheim Museum, New York, New York, *Transformations in Sculpture*

1984 The Museum of Modern Art, New York, New York, *"Primitivism" in Twentieth-Century Art: Affinity of the Tribal and the Modern*

1983 The Solomon R. Guggenheim Museum, *Recent Acquisitions*

1982 Brattleboro Museum & Art Center, Brattleboro, Vermont, *Vermont Visions*

1980 Venice Biennale, Venice, Italy, *Drawings; The Pluralist Decade*

1979 Whitney Museum of American Art, New York, New York, *1979 Biennial Exhibition*

1977 Kassel, West Germany, *Documenta 6*

Selected Bibliography
1987 Susan M. Taylor. "7 Moon Ritual Series 1985: A New Print by Michael Singer." *Print Collector's Newsletter* 17 (January-February 1987), pp. 202-203.

1984 Corinne Robins. *The Pluralist Era: American Art, 1968-1981.* New York: Harper and Row, 1984.

1981 Peter Blum. "Michael Singer: Das Kunstwerk in der Natur-Die Natur als Kunstwerk," *du,* (Zurich, Switzerland) 6 (1981), pp. 60-70.

1975 John Russell. "Michael Singer Blends Nature with Art at a Show Here." *New York Times,* December 27, 1975, p. 11.

Selected Fellowships and Awards
1981 Fellowship, National Endowment for the Arts

1980 Building Arts Grant, National Endowment for the Arts

1977, 1976 Fellowship, John Simon Guggenheim Memorial Foundation

1974 Fellowship, National Endowment for the Arts

1972 CAPS Award, New York State Council for the Arts

1971 Theodoron Award, Solomon R. Guggenheim Museum, New York

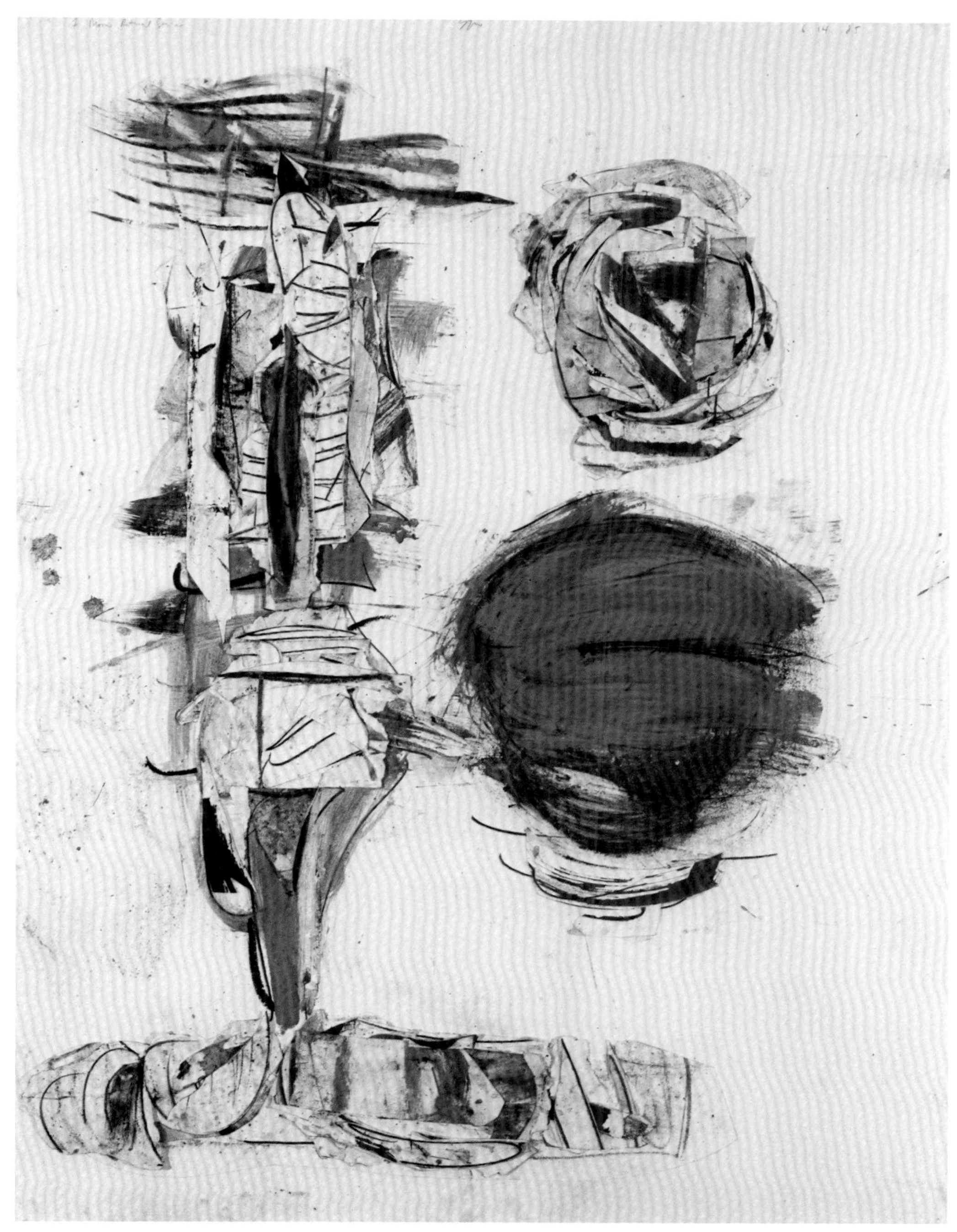

** 7 Moon Ritual Series 6.14.85,* 1985
charcoal, chalk, brush and ink,
and collage on paper
51⅜ x 39 inches
Courtesy of Sperone Westwater Gallery

7 Moon Ritual Series, 1985
lithograph and collage
51⅛ x 39½ inches
Courtesy of Sperone Westwater Gallery,
New York, New York

Michael Timpson

Out of childhood memories and the tales and poetry of his native Ireland, Michael Timpson builds environments of haunting perplexity. His imagination is unreasonable. He delights in mystery and the mythic properties of things, finding queer sympathies between reality and invention. His spaces suggest ritual precincts, closed and privileged—and strictly ordered. But their meaning is elusive or withheld altogether. Borrowing grandly, though not inappropriately, from Yeats, one feels it is here in these cryptic spaces that Timpson's ceremony of innocence is drowned.

For this exhibition the artist was commissioned by the Bowdoin College Museum of Art to design and install an environment within the oval space of the Sophia Walker Gallery. The resulting work, lyrically and inexplicably titled *Bearing the Rabbit,* is Timpson's most ambitious project to date. As in his previous projects he constructs his dream scenes from common stuff: pine boards swathed in bed linen, sacks of rice, tin pails of coal, synchronized alarm clocks, and open books illumined by bare 100-watt bulbs. Here more than before Timpson allows himself some fun: how else to explain the firmament of fluttering boxer shorts? His humor is fresh and startling—and poignant. It rounds the dark with a little light.

J.W.C.

Born 1951 in Athy, County Kildare, Ireland
Education: Center for Advanced Visual Studies, Massachusetts Institute of Technology, Cambridge, Massachusetts
Massachusetts College of Art, Boston, Massachusetts; B.F.A., 1979
University College, Dublin, Ireland
Residence: Watertown, Massachusetts

Selected Individual Exhibitions
1985, 1983 Helen Shlien Gallery, Boston, Massachusetts

1985 Bess Cutler Gallery, New York, New York

Selected Group Exhibitions
1987 The Institute of Contemporary Arts, Boston, Massachusetts, *Boston Now: Projects*

1986 Maudslay State Park, Newburyport, Massachusetts, *Art at Maudslay*

1984 The Institute of Contemporary Art, Boston, Massachusetts, *Boston Now: Sculpture*

1983 Danforth Museum, Framingham, Massachusetts, *Installation II*

The Brockton Art Museum, Brockton, Massachusetts, *Triennial Invitational*

1982 DeCordova and Dana Museum and Park, Lincoln, Massachusetts, *New Works*

1981 DeCordova and Dana Museum and Park, Lincoln, Massachusetts, *Three Installations*

Selected Bibliography
1987 Christine Temin. "The Wonder of Art and Words." *Boston Globe,* July 16, 1987, p. 13.

Lois Tarlow. "Profile: Michael Timpson." *Art New England* 8 (March 1987), pp. 14-15, 19.

1985 Nancy Stapen. "The Consumer Product and Sculpture: Michael Timpson." *Art New England* 6 (May 1985), p. 5.

Michael Brenson. "Michael Timpson." *New York Times,* February 1, 1985, p. 15.

1983 Sarah McFadden. "Report from Boston." *Art in America* 71 (May 1983), pp. 42-43.

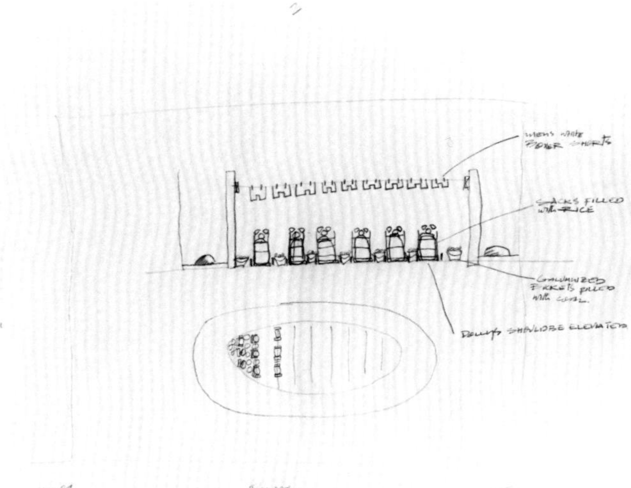

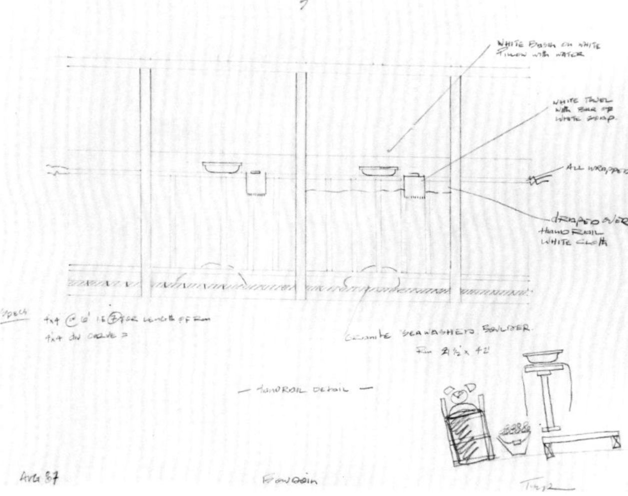

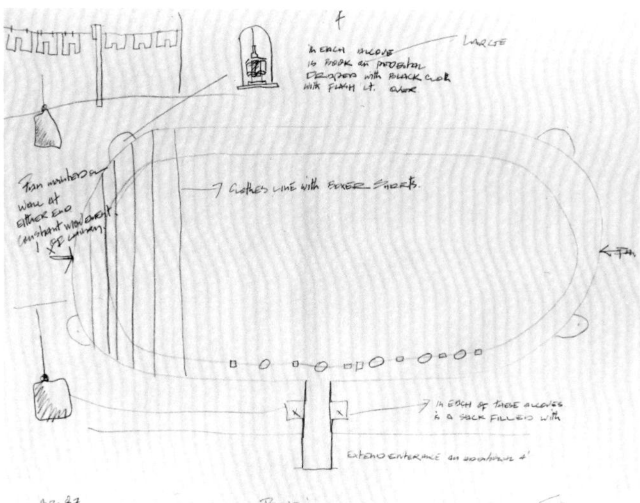

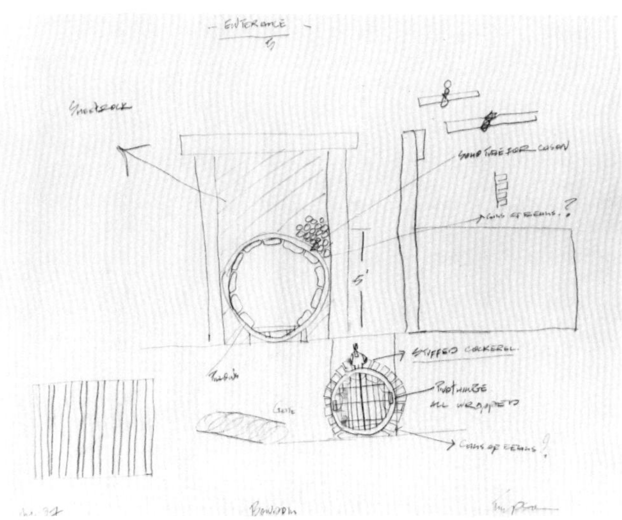

* Six preliminary drawings for
Bearing The Rabbit, 1987
graphite on paper
each sheet: 13⅞ x 17 inches
Courtesy of Stavaridis Gallery,
Boston, Massachusetts,
and Bess Cutler Gallery,
New York, New York

Bearing the Rabbit, 1988
environmental installation
Bowdoin College Museum of Art,
Brunswick, Maine

Neil Welliver

Neil Welliver's landscapes of the Maine woods have the adrenal vibrancy of a surprise encounter. They seem wholly natural and undoctored—the way it must *really* be. Only close scrutiny reveals their strict architecture and calculation. A painterly realist, Welliver does not attempt—and plainly is not interested in—the precise and uncritical transcription of nature. His art lies in the lucid interpretation of visual experience. To this end he rigorously stylizes the landscape, refashioning it into a more consistent, coherent, and oddly more convincing whole. He extracts a lyric majesty out of the rough and haphazard forms of nature and imparts meaningful structure to even the most ephemeral effects of light.

The sovereign clarity of Welliver's vision is arrived at by the application of dispassionate intelligence and disciplined technique. Welliver is the least spontaneous of artists. Although his pictures are painted with impressive authority, his confidence is that of a dancer rehearsed in the nuance of each gesture. Nothing is chanced. In numerous sketches and oil studies the artist rehearses his ideas. When the time comes to commit them to canvas all that shows is the clear and masterful performance.

J.W.C.

Born 1929 in Millville, Pennsylvania
Education: Yale School of Art, Yale University, New Haven, Connecticut; M.F.A., 1955
Philadelphia Museum College of Art, Philadelphia, Pennsylvania; B.F.A., 1953
Residence: Lincolnville, Maine
Current position: Professor of Art, University of Pennsylvania

Selected Individual Exhibitions
1987, 1985, 1983 Marlborough Gallery, New York, New York

1986 Museum of Art, Olin Art Center, Bates College, Lewiston, Maine

William A. Farnsworth Art Museum and Library, Rockland, Maine

1984 Marlborough Fine Art, London, England

1982 The Currier Gallery of Art, Manchester, New Hampshire, *Neil Welliver Paintings 1966-1980*

1981 Visual Arts Gallery, Florida International University, Tamiami, Florida, *Neil Welliver/President's Choice*

Selected Group Exhibitions
1986 The Aldrich Museum of Contemporary Art, Ridgefield, Connecticut, *A Contemporary View of Nature*

Hood Museum of Art, Dartmouth College, Hanover, New Hampshire, *Winter*

1985 Greenville County Museum of Art, Greenville, South Carolina, *Places Here and Now*

1984 Guild Hall Museum, East Hampton, New York, *Art and Friendship: A Tribute to Fairfield Porter* (traveling exhibition)

1983 The Reading Public Museum and Art Gallery, Reading, Pennsylvania, *Painted Light* (traveling exhibition)

1977 Pennsylvania Academy of the Fine Arts, Philadelphia, Pennsylvania, *Eight Contemporary Realists* (traveling exhibition)

Selected Bibliography
1987 Gerrit Henry. "Neil Welliver." *Artnews* 86 (May 1987), pp. 150-151.

1986 Avis Berman. "Artist Dialogue: Neil Welliver—Unveiling the Wilderness." *Architectural Digest* 43 (June 1986), pp. 68-78.

1985 Frank H. Goodyear, Jr. *Welliver.* New York: Rizzoli, 1985.

1984 Lois Tarlow. "Alternative Space: Neil Welliver." *Art New England* 5 (October 1984), pp. 10-11.

1983 Mark Strand, ed. *Art of the Real: Nine American Figurative Painters.* New York: Clarkson N. Potter, 1983.

Donald B. Kuspit. "Terrestrial Truth: Neil Welliver." *Art in America* 71 (April 1983), pp. 138-143.

1982 Robert Hughes. "Neil Welliver: Cold Light." *Time Magazine* 120 (October 11, 1982), p. 85.

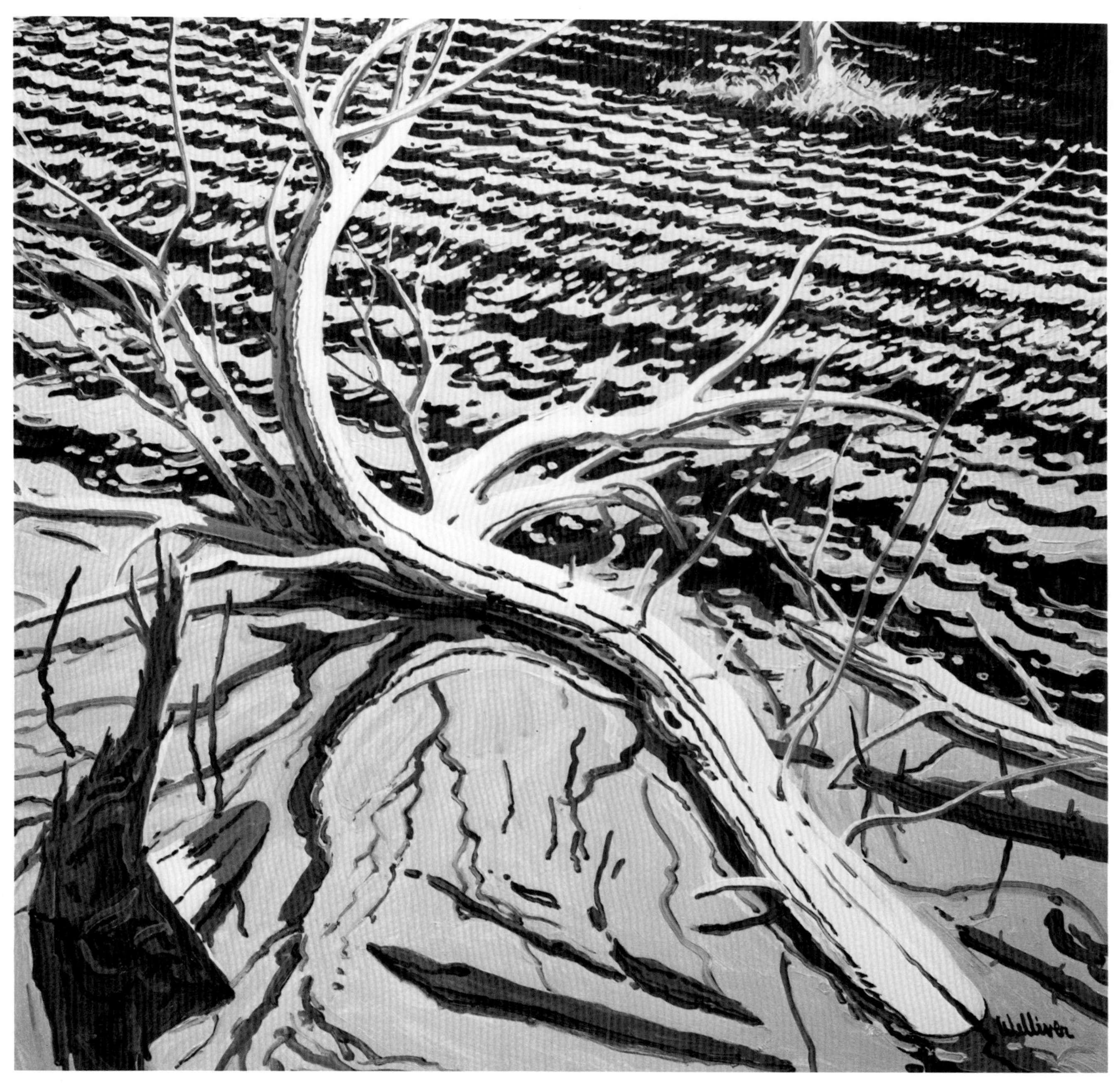

*   *Drowned Tree,* 1983
    oil on canvas
    48 x 48 inches
    Lent by Sue and David Workman

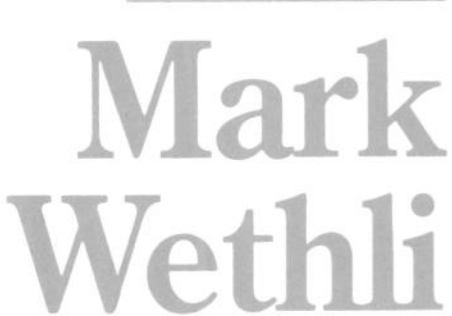

Mark Wethli

Though technically a realist, Mark Wethli has little in common with most schools of contemporary realism. His art has neither the clinical chill of photographic realism nor the nostalgic warmth of premodernist styles. It expresses a contemplative classicism which in its structure and sensibility aspires to the purity of abstraction. Reference to music is as unavoidable here as it is apt. One notes the intricacy of Wethli's compositions, their subtle balance of harmonies, livened by rhythmic phrases and the lyrical play of light. However, for all their musicality, Wethli's pictures are profoundly silent. That silence, thoughtful though not melancholy, is the true essence of his art. As in a Quaker meeting, it bestows a blessed solitude. Intimacies are further enhanced by the small scale and precise rendering of the images, which invite closer and repeated scrutiny. In these pictures Wethli transforms informal studio and domestic interiors into sanctuaries. One *enters* them not as an intruder but as an invited guest. Within them time narrows to a sustained and exquisite moment.

J.W.C.

Born 1949 in Westfield, New York
Education: University of Miami, Miami,
Florida; B.F.A., 1971; M.F.A., 1973
Residence: Brunswick, Maine
Current position: Associate Professor
and Director of Studio Art, Bowdoin
College

Selected Individual Exhibitions

1987, 1985 Koplin Gallery, Los Angeles, California

1980 Art Space Gallery, Los Angeles, California

1977 University of Northern Iowa, Cedar Falls, Iowa

1973 Corcoran & Corcoran Gallery, Miami, Florida

Selected Group Exhibitions

1987 Tatistcheff Gallery, New York, New York, *Ten Gallery Artists*

1985 Koplin Gallery, Los Angeles, California, *Interior/Exterior*

1984 Modernism Gallery, San Francisco, California, *California Drawing*

1983 Laguna Beach Museum of Art, Laguna Beach, California, *West Coast Realism* (traveling exhibition)

1980 The Brooklyn Museum, Brooklyn, New York, *American Drawings in Black & White: 1970-1980*

1977 Nancy Hoffman Gallery, New York, New York, *Summer Invitational*

1975 Whitney Museum of American Art, New York, New York, *Biennial Exhibition*

Selected Bibliography

1987 Kristine McKenna. "The Galleries," *Los Angeles Times,* May 15, 1987, p. 12.

1986 Edgar Allen Beem. "Among New England's Best." *Maine Times,* November 21, 1986, pp. 1B-7B.

1984 Robert McDonald. "Surveying Drawing in California." *Artweek* (Oakland, California), January 21, 1984, p. 12.

1980 Hilton Kramer. "American Drawings of the 70s at Brooklyn," *New York Times,* November 28, 1980, C1-C18.

Selected Fellowships and Awards

1983 Residency Fellowship, MacDowell Colony, Peterborough, New Hampshire

Residency Fellowship, Millay Colony for the Arts, Austerlitz, New York

1974 Fellowship, National Endowment for the Arts

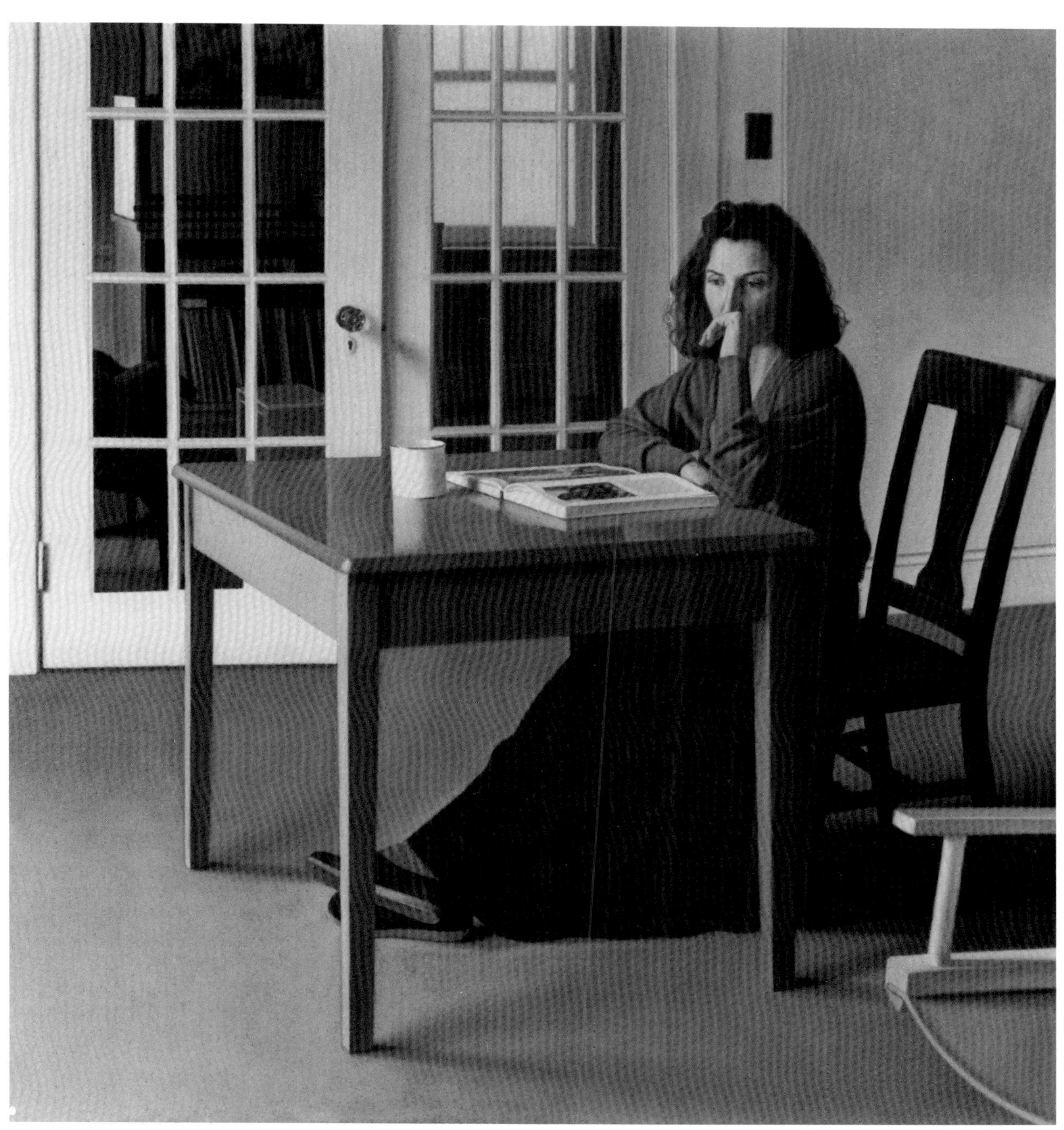

** Alice Reading,* 1986-87
oil on board
8⅝ x 8 inches
Lent by Lee Ramer,
Los Angeles, California

Radiator, 1986-87
oil on board
9 x 8 inches
Private collection

And She Was, 1986-87
oil on board
9 x 8 inches
Courtesy of Koplin Gallery,
Los Angeles, California

Philip Wofford

Philip Wofford came to Vermont in 1969 to teach painting at Bennington College after eleven years in New York City. Working in Vermont gradually brought a change in his art. While continuing to remain abstract, his paintings convey a stronger sense of place and a closer identification with landscape. The work evolved through the use of symbolic and figural elements which have changed in recent years to abstract forms suggestive of totemic presences.

He sees the process of painting as a journey filled with mostly unfamiliar images, at times highly charged with symbolic import. The ceremonial aspect of his works reveals his struggle to come to terms with the transmutability of experience and existence. A larger-than-life sensibility is evident in the scale of his painting, his use of bold, expressionistic colors, the energized compositions, and the high impasto and textural application of pigment.

His heroic, large-scale paintings of today have evolved from his early abstract, highly gestural expressionism inspired by Jackson Pollock's work of the mid-to-late 1940s, tempered by motifs and imagery of both Western and non-Western cultures. He was strongly affected by a 1968 trip to the Southwest and a love of African and Indian music, which interested him in using figurative elements reminiscent of Native American, New Guinea, and Pre-Columbian motifs.

Philip Wofford is also a published poet. Unifying his work over the years is a conception of his painting as analogous to his poetry. For him, painting functions as metaphor in its ability to express a mythic world view through emotively evocative personal imagery.

I.H.

Born 1935 in Van Buren, Arkansas
Education: University of Arkansas; B.A., 1957
University of California, Berkeley, California; 1957-1958
Residence: Hoosick Falls, New York, and Bennington, Vermont
Current position: Member of the art faculty, Bennington College, Bennington, Vermont

Selected Individual Exhibitions
1986, 1983, 1981, 1979 Nancy Hoffman Gallery, New York

1982 Carnegie Institute, Pittsburgh, Pennsylvania

1976, 1974, 1972 André Emmerich Gallery, New York

1975 Bennington College, Bennington, Vermont

1973 Yale University Art Gallery, New Haven, Connecticut

1972 The Corcoran Gallery of Art, Washington, D.C.

1962 Green Gallery, New York, New York

Selected Group Exhibitions
1987, 1986 Cranbrook Academy of Art Museum, Bloomfield Hills, Michigan, *Viewpoint 86 Painting and the Third Dimension*

1984 Robert Hull Fleming Museum, University of Vermont, Burlington, Vermont, *Contemporary Artists in Vermont*

1981 The Museum of Modern Art, New York, New York, *New Art II: Surfaces/Textures*

1978 The Brooklyn Museum, Brooklyn, New York, *Recent Acquisitions*

1976 Robert Hull Fleming Museum, University of Vermont, Burlington, Vermont, *Vermont Landscape Images*

1975, 1973 The Corcoran Gallery of Art, Washington, D.C., *Biennial of American Painting*

1972, 1969 Whitney Museum of American Art, New York, New York, *Biennial Exhibition*

Selected Bibliography
1986 Donald B. Kuspit. "Philip Wofford at Nancy Hoffman." *Art in America* 74 (May 1986), pp. 163-165.

1983 Ronny H. Cohen. "The New Paintings of Philip Wofford." *Arts Magazine* 58 (November 1983), pp. 133-135.

1982 Debra Bricker Balken. "An Interview with Philip Wofford." *Arts Magazine* 57 (December 1982), pp. 87-89.

1970 Carter Ratcliff. "New Informalists." *Artnews* 68 (February 1970), pp. 46-50.

1962 Sidney Tillim. "New York Exhibitions: In the Galleries: Philip Wofford." *Arts Magazine* 37 (December 1962), p. 49.

Selected Fellowships and Awards
1986 Fellowship, John Simon Guggenheim Memorial Foundation

1980, 1975, 1974 Fellowship, National Endowment for the Arts

1978, 1977 CAPS Fellowship, New York State Council on the Arts

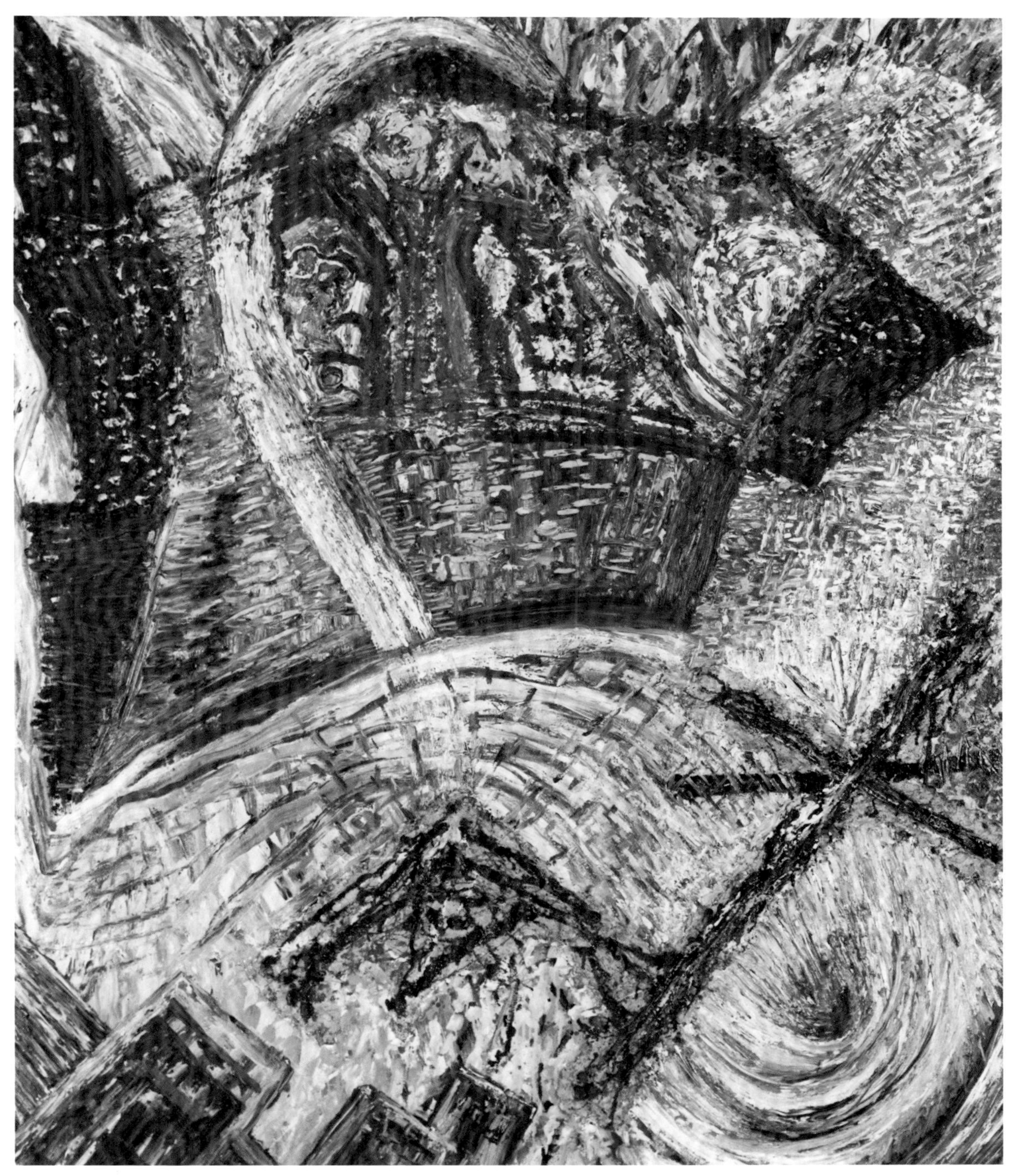

* *Second Transmigration*, 1986
acrylic and oil on canvas
63 x 58 inches
Lent by the artist